D1431510

H

CHINESE
pocket
GRAMMAR
AND SCRIPT

New York Chicago San Francisco Lisbon London Madrid Mexico City
Milan New Delhi San Juan Seoul Singapore Sydney Toronto

ISBN 978-0-07-163624-7
MHID 0-07-163624-2

McGraw-Hill books are available at special quantity discounts to use as
premiums and sales promotions or for use in corporate training programs.
To contact a representative, please visit the Contact Us pages at
www.mhprofessional.com.

Authors: Michelle Hsu McWilliam, Maggie Sproule
Project Editors: Alex Hepworth, Kate Nicholson
With Helen Bleck

Designed by Chambers Harrap Publishers Ltd, Edinburgh
Typeset in Rotis Serif and Meta Plus by Macmillan Publishing Solutions

INTRODUCTION

This Chinese grammar from Chambers has been written to meet the needs of all students of Mandarin Chinese, and is particularly useful for those taking school examinations. The essential rules of the Chinese language have been set out in terms that are as accessible as possible to all users. Where technical terms have been used, full explanations of these terms have also been supplied. There is also a glossary of grammatical terminology on **pages 7-12**.

The emphasis has been placed squarely on modern spoken Chinese. This grammar, with its wealth of lively and typical illustrations of usage taken from the present-day language, is the ideal study tool for all levels – from the beginner who is starting to get to grips with the Chinese language through to the advanced user who requires a comprehensive and readily accessible work of reference.

In this book, simplified Chinese characters appear first and are followed by their pinyin transcriptions. A full list of Chinese radicals is provided on **pages 153-60**. This brand-new book also boasts a smart colour design to make consultation even easier and more enjoyable.

CONTENTS

	GLOSSARY OF GRAMMATICAL TERMS	7
1.	CHINESE SCRIPT	13
	A. The Chinese language	13
	B. The Chinese writing system	13
	C. Chinese characters	14
	D. Pinyin	20
	E. Tones	20
	F. Punctuation	21
2.	WORD ORDER	22
	A. Structures similar to English	22
	B. Structures different from English	22
3.	NEGATIVE EXPRESSIONS	25
	A. 不 **bù**	25
	B. 没 **méi**	26
	C. 别 **bié**	27
4.	QUESTIONS AND QUESTION WORDS	28
	A. Forming yes/no questions	28
	B. Question words	29
5.	NOUNS	41
	A. Common nouns	41
	B. Proper nouns	42
	C. Noun phrases	43
6.	PRONOUNS	45
	A. Personal pronouns	45
	B. The reflexive pronoun 自己 **zìjǐ**	47
	C. Possessive pronouns	48
	D. Relative pronouns	49
	E. Demonstrative pronouns	50
7.	ADJECTIVES	52
	A. Attributive adjectives	52
	B. Adjectival stative verbs	53

8.	ADVERBS	56
A.	Types of adverb	56
B.	Position of the adverb	62
C.	Modifying adjectives	63
D.	Some particular cases	63
9.	IMPERATIVES AND EXCLAMATIVES	67
A.	Imperatives	67
B.	Exclamatives	70
10.	VERBS	73
A.	Stative verbs	73
B.	Modal verbs	75
C.	Action verbs	79
11.	COMPLEMENTS	88
A.	Complements of degree	88
B.	Complements of result	89
C.	Directional complements	92
D.	Potential complements	93
12.	PREPOSITIONS	95
A.	Position of prepositions	95
B.	Prepositions of time and location	96
C.	Some particular cases	99
D.	Disyllabic prepositions	103
E.	Passive voice	105
13.	CONJUNCTIONS	106
A.	Coordinating conjunctions	106
B.	Correlative conjunctions	109
C.	Cohesive conjunctions	110
D.	Subordinating conjunctions	113
14.	NUMBERS AND QUANTITY	117
A.	Cardinal numbers	117
B.	Ordinal numbers	119
C.	Mathematical expressions	120
D.	Approximate numbers	122
15.	EXPRESSIONS OF QUANTITY	124
A.	Measure words	124
B.	Other expressions of quantity	131

CONTENTS

16. EXPRESSIONS OF TIME 133
    A. The date 133
    B. The time 135
17. COMPARISON 138
    A. Positive comparison 138
    B. Negative comparison 140
    C. Similarity 141
    D. Superlative 142
    E. Constructions with 越 yuè ... 越 yuè 143
18. LOCATION AND DIRECTION 146
    A. Location words 146
    B. Direction words 148
    C. Expressions of location with 在 zài and 有 yǒu 151
19. LIST OF RADICALS 153
INDEX 163

GLOSSARY OF GRAMMATICAL TERMS

ACTIVE   The active form of a verb is the basic form, as in **I** **remember** her. It is normally opposed to the PASSIVE form of the verb as in **she *will be remembered***.

ACTION VERB   Action verbs are used to express activities that have a fixed duration. Unlike stative verbs, they cannot express a continued state. *See also* VERB *and* STATIVE VERB.

ADJECTIVAL STATIVE VERB   Some verbs in Chinese are translated as English adjectives. These are known as adjectival stative verbs and function as both the verb, usually **to be**, and the adjective.

ADJECTIVE   An adjective provides extra information about a noun. Adjectives that appear before a noun are called attributive adjectives, eg **a *small* house**. Adjectives that appear after a noun are called predicative adjectives, eg **the house is *small***. In Chinese, predicative adjectives function as verbs. *See also* ADJECTIVAL STATIVE VERB.

ADVERB   Adverbs are normally used with a verb to add extra information by indicating ***how*** the action is done, ***when***, ***where*** and with ***how much intensity*** the action is done, or ***to what extent*** the action is done. Adverbs may also be used with an adjective or another adverb, eg **a *very* attractive girl**, ***very* well**.

ASPECT MARKER   In Chinese, verbs do not change their form depending on the tense as they do in English, eg **go/went/gone**. Instead, the time at which an action takes place can be indicated by one of the aspect markers le, guò or zhe. These indicate whether an action is completed or ongoing and are often used with expressions of time.

CARDINAL   Cardinal numbers are numbers such as **one, two, ten, fourteen,** as opposed to ORDINAL numbers (eg **first, second**).

CLAUSE   A clause is a group of words that contains at least a subject and a verb: **he said** is a clause. A clause often contains more than this basic information, eg *he said* **this to her yesterday.** Sentences can be made up of several clauses, eg **he said/he'd call me/ if he were free.** *See* SENTENCE.

COMPARATIVE   The comparative forms of adjectives and adverbs allow us to compare two things, people or actions. In English, **more ... than, ...er than, less ... than** and **as ... as** are used for comparison. The comparative is usually indicated with bǐ in Chinese.

CONDITIONAL   This mood is used to describe what someone would do, or something that would happen, if a condition was fulfilled. In English it is usually expressed with **if** and in Chinese with rúguǒ.

CONJUNCTION   Conjunctions are used to link different CLAUSES. Conjunctions in Chinese can be coordinating (**and, but, also**), correlative (**both ... and, not only ... but also**), cohesive (**therefore, then**) or subordinating (**because, unless**).

DEMONSTRATIVE   Demonstrative adjectives such as **this, that, these** are used to point out a particular person or object.

DIRECT OBJECT   A direct object is a noun or a pronoun which in English follows a verb without any linking preposition, eg **I met** *a friend.* Note that in English a preposition is often omitted, eg in **I sent him a present, him** is equivalent to **to him** and **a present** is the direct object.

EXCLAMATION   An exclamation is a word or sentence used to express surprise, annoyance *etc*, eg **what!, wow!, how lucky!, what a nice day!**

IMPERATIVE   This mood is used for giving orders, eg **stop!, don't go!** or for making suggestions, eg **let's go.**

INDIRECT OBJECT   An indirect object is a pronoun or noun which follows a verb indirectly, sometimes with a linking preposition (usually **to**), eg **I spoke to** *my friend/him*, **she gave** *him* **a kiss**.

INFINITIVE   The infinitive is the basic form of the verb as found in dictionaries, eg **to eat, to finish, to take**. In Chinese the verb only has one form.

INTERROGATIVE   Interrogative words are used to ask a question and usually begin with *wh-* in English (**who, what, where** *etc*).

MEASURE WORD   In Chinese, nouns cannot be quantified by a numeral alone. A specific measure word must be used between the numeral and the noun. There are hundreds of measure words in use, but the most common is ge.

MODAL VERB   Modal verbs are used before another verb to provide additional information about an action, for example to express obligation, permission or need.

NOUN   A noun is a word or a group of words which refers to a living creature, a thing, a place or an abstract idea, eg **postman, cat, shop, passport, life**.

NUMBER   The number of a noun indicates whether the noun is singular or plural. A singular noun refers to one single thing or person, eg **boy, train** and a plural noun to more than one, eg **boys, trains**. In Chinese, number is marked by a measure word. *See also* MEASURE WORD.

OBJECT   *See* DIRECT OBJECT, INDIRECT OBJECT.

ORDINAL   Ordinal numbers are **first, second, third, fourth** *etc*.

PASSIVE   A verb is used in the passive when the subject of the verb does not perform the action but is subjected to it. The passive is often formed with a part of the verb **to be** and the past participle of the verb, eg **he was rewarded**. In Chinese the passive is most frequently formed with the preposition bèi. *See also* ACTIVE.

PAST PARTICIPLE   The past participle of a verb is the form that is used after **to have** in English, eg **he/she has** *eaten* **some noodles**. In Chinese the past tense is indicated by context, an expression of time or by an aspect marker. *See also* ASPECT MARKER.

PERSON   In any tense, there are three persons in the singular (1st: **I ...**, 2nd: **you ...**, 3rd: **he/she/it ...**), and three in the plural (1st: **we ...**, 2nd: **you ...**, 3rd: **they ...**).

PERSONAL PRONOUNS   Personal pronouns stand for a noun. They usually accompany a verb and can be either the SUBJECT (**I, you, he/she/it, we, they**) or the OBJECT of the verb (**me, you, him/her/it, us, them**). In Chinese, personal pronouns are the same whether they are the subject or the object of the verb.

PINYIN   This is a system of phonetic writing using Roman letters, created to make Chinese characters easier to learn. In this book, all examples given in Chinese characters will be followed by a pinyin transcription.

PLURAL   *See* NUMBER.

POSSESSIVE   Possessive adjectives like **my, your, our** and possessive pronouns like **mine, yours, ours** are used to indicate possession or ownership. In Chinese there is no distinction between possessive adjectives and possessive pronouns.

PREPOSITION   Prepositions are words such as **with, in, to, at**; in English they are followed by a noun or a pronoun. Prepositions are sometimes known as 'coverbs' in Chinese, because they are almost always used with a verb.

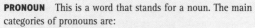

PRONOUN   This is a word that stands for a noun. The main categories of pronouns are:

- ❏ *Relative pronouns* (eg **who, which, that**)
- ❏ *Interrogative pronouns* (eg **who?, what?, which?**)
- ❏ *Demonstrative pronouns* (eg **this, that, these**)
- ❏ *Possessive pronouns* (eg **mine, yours, his**)
- ❏ *Personal pronouns* (eg **you, him, us**)
- ❏ *Reflexive pronouns* (eg **myself, himself**)
- ❏ *Indefinite pronouns* (eg **something, all**)

REFLEXIVE   Reflexive verbs 'reflect' the action back onto the subject, eg **I** dressed **myself**. They are always found with a reflexive pronoun, eg **myself**, **herself** *etc*. In Chinese there is only one reflexive pronoun, zìjǐ.

SENTENCE   A sentence is a group of words made up of one or more CLAUSES and forming a complete grammatical structure. The end of a sentence is indicated by a punctuation mark (usually a full stop, a question mark or an exclamation mark).

SINGULAR   *See* NUMBER.

STATIVE VERB   A stative verb describes a prolonged state, such as someone's profession or nationality, or a situation whereby no obvious action takes place, eg **I** *like* **this book**, **he** *understands* **maths**. Some stative verbs in Chinese are translated as adjectives in English. *See* ADJECTIVAL STATIVE VERB.

SUBJECT   The subject of a verb is the noun or pronoun that performs the action. In the sentences *the train* **left early** and *she* **bought a CD**, **the train** and **she** are the subjects.

SUPERLATIVE   The form of an adjective or an adverb which, in English, is marked by **the most ...**, **the ...est** or **the least ...**. In Chinese, the superlative is formed by placing zuì before an adjective.

TENSE In English, different forms of the verb are used in tenses, which tell us when an action takes place, eg in the present, the past, the future. In Chinese, tenses are instead indicated by context, an expression of time or by an aspect marker. *See also* ASPECT MARKER.

TONE Chinese is a tonal language and has four tones, as well as a neutral tone, which can alter according to the subsequent syllable. Tone is only marked in pinyin transcriptions, not in Chinese characters. *See also* PINYIN.

TOPICALIZATION In Chinese a CLAUSE may be brought to the beginning of a sentence to emphasize it. This is known as topicalization.

VERB A verb is a word which usually describes an action, eg **to sing, to work, to watch**, or the existence of a state, eg **to be, to have, to hope**. *See also* ACTION VERB *and* STATIVE VERB.

VOICE The two voices of a verb are its ACTIVE and PASSIVE forms.

1 CHINESE SCRIPT

A THE CHINESE LANGUAGE

The Chinese language is called 汉语 hànyǔ (language of the Han people, the Han being the majority ethnic group in China). It is also sometimes called 普通话 pǔtōnghuà, meaning common or standard language. This is the language spoken in the central and northern regions of China, and is based especially on the language of Beijing. In the West, it is often known as Mandarin Chinese. It is the official language, and the language used in education and in the media.

In the south of China, other dialects are often spoken, but Mandarin Chinese is the common language understood by all Chinese people. In the provinces of Canton and Hong Kong most people speak Cantonese, but Mandarin is, even there, increasingly becoming the language of business.

B THE CHINESE WRITING SYSTEM

The Chinese writing system is essentially a picture language; this means that it is not alphabetic but rather is based on a system of characters. The history of written Chinese dates back over 6,000 years. Originally, primitive drawings were used to represent objects and ideas and these drawings evolved into Chinese characters. In ancient times, many local variations of scripts were used, but over time they became standardized throughout the empire, and the structure and key elements of the system are still used today in the written language.

This writing system represents ideas, not sounds. As there is no alphabet connecting the writing to its pronunciation, there are no direct clues as to how each character should be pronounced. Although there is no explicit relation between written Chinese and its pronunciation, many Chinese characters do have phonetic or sound elements. However, because of regional dialect variations and changes over time, these elements can be somewhat unreliable.

C CHINESE CHARACTERS

There are two sources to explain the origin and evolution of the Chinese writing system: one is based on legends as described in ancient Chinese texts, and the other is based on archaeological findings, such as the inscriptions on oracle bones and bronze vessels.

1 General points

Each Chinese character is constructed out of simple lines, commonly known as strokes. Each character is made up of one or more strokes grouped together in a fairly uniform square block, hence the term 'square-block characters'. Knowledge of 3,000-4,000 characters is generally enough to be able to read a Chinese newspaper.

In Chinese, each character represents a single unit of meaning and a single segment of speech. The characters themselves never change, unlike in English, where words can have different endings to show number or tense. A good number of characters are fairly memorable because it is easy to make connections between the characters and the objects they represent.

2 Traditional and simplified characters

In the mid-1950s, the Communist Chinese government began promoting a simplified writing system in an effort to boost China's literacy rate. During the process of simplification, over 1,000 characters were eliminated and the number of strokes in many characters reduced. Today, the simplified characters are used in most regions of China, although the traditional or full forms are still used as standard in Taiwan and many overseas Chinese communities. For example:

English	Traditional characters	Simplified characters
country	國	国
to learn	學習	学习
to listen	聽	听
to speak	說	说

3 Strokes

Chinese characters are written using simple lines, known as strokes. There are eight basic strokes:

Stroke	Name
㇔	dot
一	horizontal
丨	vertical
丿	sweep to the left
㇏	sweep to the right
㇀	rising (almost like a tick)
亅	hook
㇕	horizontal turn

4 How to form characters

The different strokes are combined to form characters. Generally speaking, a character may consist of one, two or three parts, and these parts are arranged in a fashion that fits into a block-like shape.

Basic structure	Form	Examples
Single-component characters		人
Left – right		好
		川
		唱
		部
Top – bottom		二
Top – middle – bottom		意 → 立 / 日 / 心
Top – left – right		花 → 艹 / 人 匕
Left – right – bottom		想 → 木 目 / 心
Inside – outside		国 → 口 + 玉
Symmetrical		小

5 Main categories of characters

Chinese characters can be broadly divided into the following four categories:

a) Pictograms

These characters are representative symbols; the character resembles the object it represents. For example:

sun	日
moon	月
mountain	山
water/river	水
wood/tree	木
fire	火
person	人

b) Ideograms

Like pictograms, these are symbols; ideograms convey ideas and abstract concepts. For example, in the character 旦 the 日 represents the sun, and the 一 indicates the horizon. With the sun emerging above the horizon, the character 旦 means 'dawn'. Here are a few examples of ideograms:

middle	中
above	上
under	下

c) Associative compounds

In Chinese, two or more pictograms or ideograms are combined to create a new character and hence a new meaning. For example, the characters 日 (sun) and 月 (moon) are combined to create the character 明, which means 'bright'.

Here are some more examples of associative compounds:

good	女 woman + 子 child	好
to rest	人 person + 木 wood	休
to see	手 hand + 目 eye	看

d) Semantic-phonetic compounds

Semantic-phonetic compounds combine a pictogram, indicating the general meaning of the character, and a phonetic indicator to provide a clue to the pronunciation. For example, the word for 'mother', 妈 mā, is composed of the character 女 nǚ (woman) on the left and the character 马 mǎ (horse) on the right. As 马 is pronounced mǎ, it indicates that the pronunciation of 妈 mā is similar to 马 mǎ. This group represents approximately 85 percent of all Chinese characters. Here are some more examples:

Character	Semantic + phonetic components	Pronunciation	Meaning
情	忄 heart + 青 qīng	qíng	feelings, emotions
请	讠 speech + 青 qīng	qǐng	request, invite; please
睛	目 eye + 青 qīng	jīng	eye
清	氵 water + 青 qīng	qīng	clear

6 Radicals

For a list of Chinese radicals, see **pages 153–60.**

The radical is the 'root' of a word, that is, the basis of its meaning. For example, 女 nǚ (woman) is the radical in 妈 mā (mother), 姐 jiě (elder sister), 妹 mèi (younger sister) and 她 tā (she). The presence of the same radical in all these characters indicates that they are all associated in meaning with 女 nǚ. These characters will all be listed under the radical 女 nǚ in the dictionary.

For example:

Radical	English meaning	Example	English
人/亻	person	你 nǐ	you
口	mouth	吃 chī	to eat
女	female	妈 mā	mother
日	sun	明 míng	bright
木	wood	林 lín	tree
火/灬	fire	烤 kǎo	to roast
目	eye	看 kàn	to see
言/讠	speech	语 yǔ	language

7 Combining characters to make words

Many Chinese words are formed by combining two separate characters. Here are some examples:

电 diàn	electricity
电脑 diànnǎo	electricity + brain = computer
电视 diànshì	electricity + vision = television
电话 diànhuà	electricity + words = telephone

火 huǒ	fire
火山 huǒshān	fire + mountain = volcano
火车 huǒchē	fire + vehicle = train
火气 huǒqì	fire + breath = temper

D PINYIN

In 1958, the People's Republic of China adopted a system of phonetic writing using Roman letters, with the aim of making the characters easier to learn. This transcription system is known as 拼音 pīnyīn ('pinyin'). While some older Chinese people are not familiar with it, young people use this system when they learn Chinese, and it is extremely helpful to foreign learners.

In this book, each phrase in English will have a translation using simplified Chinese characters and will also be followed by its equivalent in pinyin, based on approximations to English-language sounds familiar to the reader.

E TONES

Chinese has four tones, as well as a neutral tone. These tones convey differences in meaning and pronouncing a syllable with the wrong tone can give rise to confusion. Although tones are not marked in the characters, they are written in pinyin as accents above the main vowel of each syllable and act as a guide to pronunciation. An unmarked syllable is neutral and unstressed.

In the diagrams below, the vertical line shows the range of pitch of our voices. The diagrams should help you to understand how to produce the tones.

First tone   high |————————→

ā

High-pitched and steady

Second tone

á

Starting low and rising

Third tone

ǎ

Starting around middle pitch, falling and then rising

Fourth tone

à

Starting high and falling

Examples:

妈 mā (mother) first tone: flat, but quite high pitch.

麻 má (hemp) second tone: rising, starting low, ending on a high pitch.

马 mǎ (horse) third tone: falling-rising.

骂 mà (to swear) fourth tone: falling.

吗 ma (marks a question): unstressed.

F PUNCTUATION

Most punctuation in Chinese is very similar to European punctuation. Exclamation marks, question marks, semi-colons, colons and brackets all look roughly like their European equivalents. The two main exceptions are the comma and the full stop.

1 Comma

There are two types of comma in Chinese: the first is the same as that used in English, and the second is the enumerative comma: 、. The enumerative comma must be used when listing items, for example:

中国 Zhōngguó (China)、美国 Měiguó (USA)、日本 Rìběn (Japan)、法国 Fǎguó (France)、德国 Déguó (Germany).

2 Full stop

A full stop in Chinese is indicated by a small circle: 。

2 WORD ORDER

Word order is extremely important in Chinese, given that the characters do not change to show the grammatical relations between words in a sentence. Although in many respects Chinese word order is quite different from the English, there are a few key structures where the word order follows the same pattern.

A STRUCTURES SIMILAR TO ENGLISH

1 Subject-verb-object

他吃汉堡包
tā chī hànbǎobāo
he eats hamburgers

我喜欢这个电影
wǒ xǐhuān zhè ge diànyǐng
I like this movie

2 Adjective before noun

好天气
hǎo tiānqì
<u>good</u> weather

漂亮的花
piàoliàng de huā
<u>pretty</u> flowers

For more information on the position of adjectives, see pages 52-4.

B STRUCTURES DIFFERENT FROM ENGLISH

1 Subject + time and/or location + verb

我三点看书
wǒ <u>sān diǎn</u> kànshū
(*lit.* I <u>three o'clock</u> read book)
I was reading a book at three o'clock

我在家看书
wǒ <u>zài jiā</u> kànshū
(*lit.* I <u>at home</u> read book)
I was at home reading a book

我三点在家看书
wǒ sān diǎn zài jiā kànshū
(*lit.* I three o'clock at home read book)
at three o'clock, I was at home reading a book

However, when referring to a period of time, rather than a specific point in time, the verb is placed *before* the time period that complements it, as in English. *See also* **pages 80-7**.

我看书看了三个小时
wǒ kànshū kàn le sān ge xiǎoshí
I've been reading a book for three hours

2 Preposition before verb

爸爸为我买了一个电脑
bàba wèi wǒ mǎi-le yí ge diànnǎo
(*lit.* Dad for me bought a computer)
Dad bought me a computer

See **pages 95-6** *for more on the position of prepositions.*

3 Topicalization

Topicalization refers to moving the 'topic' of the sentence, that is the most important element, to the beginning in order to emphasize it. In the first example below, the emphasis is on 'this movie', so it comes first in the sentence. However, if the emphasis is moved to 'we', then the word order changes, as in the second example below:

这个电影，我们都看过
zhè ge diànyǐng, wǒmen dōu kàn-guò
(*lit.* this movie, we've already watched)
we've already watched *this movie*

我们都看过这个电影
wǒmen dōu kàn-guò zhè ge diànyǐng
(*lit.* we've already watched this movie)
we've already watched this movie

4 Sentences with 有 yǒu

有 yǒu is equivalent to 'there is/there are' and typically occurs between the location of the object and the object itself. *See also* page 74.

花园里有很多树
huāyuán lǐ <u>yǒu</u> hěn duō shù
(*lit.* in the garden <u>there are</u> many trees)
there are many trees in the garden

桌子上有两杯咖啡
zhuōzi shàng <u>yǒu</u> liǎng bēi kāfēi
(*lit.* on the table <u>there are</u> two cups of coffee)
there are two cups of coffee on the table

5 No impersonal pronoun 'it'

The impersonal pronoun 'it' is commonly used in English when the action described by the verb is not carried out by a particular person or thing (for example when talking about the weather). There is no such pronoun in Chinese:

好冷！	今天很热	十点钟
hǎo lěng!	jīntiān hěn rè	shí diǎnzhōng
(*lit.* very cold!)	(*lit.* very hot today)	(*lit.* ten o'clock)
it's very cold!	**it's very hot today**	**it's ten o'clock**

3 NEGATIVE EXPRESSIONS

The most common ways to express a negative are to use the following words, all of which can be loosely translated as 'not'.

 A 不 bù

For the use of 不 bù in questions, see **pages 28-9.**

不 bù is the most common way to express a negative and is used before the verb to negate both actions and statements in the present and future, but not in the past tense.

1 Negating actions

Present
我不看电视
wǒ <u>bú</u> kàn diànshì
I'm <u>not</u> watching TV

Future
我明天不看电视
wǒ míngtiān <u>bú</u> kàn diànshì
I <u>won't</u> be watching TV tomorrow

Habitual
他总是不看电视
tā zǒngshì <u>bú</u> kàn diànshì
he <u>never</u> watches TV

2 Negating statements

你不应该看电视
nǐ bù yīnggāi kàn diànshì
you <u>should not</u> be watching TV

她不像她爸爸
tā bú xiàng tā bàba
she is <u>not like</u> her father

我不是学生
wǒ <u>bú shì</u> xuéshēng
I <u>am not</u> a student

这条河不长
zhè tiáo hé bù cháng
this river is <u>not long</u>

 B 没 méi

1 With the verb 有 yǒu to negate possession

The verb 有 yǒu (to have) can only be negated by 没 méi – *never* by 不 bù. Thus 没有 méiyǒu can be roughly interpreted as 'not have', 'don't have'. For example:

我没有钱
wǒ <u>méiyǒu</u> qiǎn
I <u>don't have</u> any money

Note, however, that 没 méi is often used alone as an abbreviation for 没有 méiyǒu.

2 To negate an action in the past

没有 méiyǒu is placed before a verb to negate an action in the past. Note that 没有 méiyǒu and its abbreviated form 没 méi can be used interchangeably here:

我昨天没看电视
wǒ zuótiān <u>méi</u> kàn diànshì
I <u>didn't</u> watch TV yesterday

我没去过中国
wǒ <u>méi</u> qù-guò Zhōngguó
I <u>have not</u> been to China

C 别 **bié**

For more on the use of 别 bié *as an imperative see also* **page 69.**

The negative imperative is formed by placing 别 bié in front of the verb and can be used in two ways.

1 To express 'don't!'

别说话!
bié shuōhuà!
<u>don't</u> talk!

别告诉别人!
bié gàosù biérén!
<u>don't</u> tell anyone!

2 To express 'stop!'

别 bié is used with the particle 了 le to express 'stop ...ing!' *For the other uses of* 了 le *see* **pages 80-3.**

别说话了!
bié shuōhuà le!
<u>stop</u> talking!

别吃了!
bié chī le!
<u>stop</u> eating!

4 QUESTIONS AND QUESTION WORDS

A FORMING YES/NO QUESTIONS

There are three main ways to form yes/no questions in Chinese.

1 With the question particle 吗 ma

The question particle 吗 ma may be added to the end of a statement. Note that this does not affect the word order. For example:

她是学生
tā shì xuéshēng → 她是学生吗?
she is a student

tā shì xuéshēng ma?
is she a student?

2 With the construction 'verb + 不 bù + verb'

In this construction the verb must be given in both the positive and negative to form a question:

他喜欢足球
tā xǐhuān zúqiú → 他喜欢不喜欢足球?
he likes football

tā xǐhuān bù xǐhuān zúqiú?
(*lit.* he likes not likes football?)
does he like football?

If the verb has more than one syllable, then the first (positive) occurrence of the verb can be shortened to one syllable, for example:

妈妈很高兴
Māma hěn gāoxìng → 妈妈高不高兴?
Mum is very happy

Māma gāo bù gāoxìng?
is Mum happy?

Note that 不 bù cannot be used in this way to form questions with the verb 有 yǒu (to have). When forming questions with 有 yǒu, it is necessary to use the construction '有 yǒu + 没 méi + 有 yǒu' (*see* page 26).

学校没有礼堂
xuéxiào méiyǒu lǐtáng   →
the school doesn't have a hall

学校有没有礼堂?
xuéxiào <u>yǒu méiyǒu</u> lǐtáng?
<u>does</u> the school <u>have</u> a hall?

3 With 是否 shìfǒu

是否 shìfǒu (whether) can be used before a verb to construct a more formal question:

我不知道你是否听过这个人?
wǒ bù zhīdào nǐ <u>shìfǒu</u> tīng-guò zhè ge rén?
I don't know <u>whether</u> you have heard of this person (<u>or not</u>)?

> *Note*
>
> In Chinese, these types of questions cannot actually be answered with 'yes' or 'no'. Instead, the positive form of the verb (eg 喜欢 xǐhuān) or the negative form of the verb (eg 不喜欢 bù xǐhuān) must be used.

B QUESTION WORDS

In the same way as the question particle 吗 ma, Chinese question words can be added to a statement to form a question. However, sentences containing question words cannot also contain 吗 ma.

Unlike in English, where the question word generally begins the sentence, in Chinese the word order remains unchanged.

The question word is simply inserted in the same position as the word that replaces it in the answer. For example:

他是我的汉语老师
tā shì wǒde Hànyǔ lǎoshī
he is my Chinese language teacher

→

他是谁?
tā shì shéi?
(*lit.* he is who?)
who is he?

1 Interrogative pronouns

谁 shéi	who, whom
谁的 shéide	whose
什么 shénme	what
哪 nǎ	which (*singular*)
哪些 nǎxiē	which (*plural*)

a) 谁 shéi can be used to express both 'who' and 'whom' in English. Note that it can also be pronounced 谁 shuí.

谁是你的汉语老师?
shéi shì nǐde Hànyǔ lǎoshī?
who is your Chinese language teacher?

b) 谁的 shéide (whose) can be used in a similar way to English, either as an interrogative noun:

这笔是谁的?
zhè bǐ shì shéide?
(*lit.* this pen is whose?)
whose is this pen?

or as an interrogative adjective + noun:

这是谁的笔?
zhè shì shéide bǐ?
(*lit.* this is whose pen?)
whose pen is this?

c) 什么 shénme can be used to express both 'what' and 'what kind of ...'

你要什么？
nǐ yào <u>shénme</u>?
(*lit.* you want <u>what</u>?)
what would you like?

你要什么炒面？
nǐ yào <u>shénme</u> chǎomiàn?
(*lit.* you want <u>what</u> fried noodles?)
what kind of fried noodles would you like?

d) 哪 nǎ (which)

你是哪国人？
nǐ shì <u>nǎ</u> guó rén?
(*lit.* you are <u>which</u> country person?)
which country are you from?

Note that when 哪 nǎ appears before a noun where a numeral is implied, it is necessary to use the appropriate measure word in the construction '哪 nǎ + measure word + noun':

你要哪本书？
nǐ yào <u>nǎ běn</u> shū?
(*lit.* you want <u>which [one]</u> book?)
which book do you want?

Where the numeral is expressed, use the construction '哪 nǎ + numeral + measure word + noun':

你要哪两本书？
nǐ yào <u>nǎ liǎng běn</u> shū?
(*lit.* you want <u>which two</u> books?)
which two books do you want?

For more on measure words see **pages 124-9.**

e) 哪些 nǎxiē can be used to express 'which' or 'which ones' where
the number is not specified:

哪些书是你的?
nǎxiē shū shì nǐde?
<u>which</u> books are yours?

2 Other question words

哪儿 nǎr	where
为什么 wèishénme	why
怎么 zěnme	how; why
怎么样 zěnmeyàng	how; how about
多 duō + adjective/adverb	how + adjective/adverb
多久 duō jiǔ	how long *(time)*
多长时间 duō cháng shíjiān	how long *(time)*
多少 duōshǎo	how much, how many
几 jǐ	how many *(where the answer is anticipated to be less than 10)*

a) 哪儿 nǎr (where) can be used in the object position:

你去哪儿?
nǐ qù <u>nǎr</u>?
(*lit.* you go <u>where</u>?)
where do you go?/where are you going?

It can also be used in a similar way to English, at the beginning
of a question:

哪儿有银行?
<u>nǎr</u> yǒu yínháng?
(*lit.* <u>where</u> has bank?)
where can I find a bank?

and in the constructions '在 zài (in, at, on) + 哪儿 nǎr + verb'
and '到 dào (to) + 哪儿 nǎr + verb':

他弟弟在哪儿学习？
tā dìdi zài nǎr xuéxí?
(*lit.* his younger brother <u>at where</u> studying?)
where is his younger brother studying?

明天我们到哪儿去？
míngtiān wǒmen dào nǎr qù?
(*lit.* tomorrow we <u>to where</u> go?)
where are we going tomorrow?

b) 为什么 wèishénme (why)

你为什么来英国？
nǐ <u>wèishénme</u> lái Yīngguó?
<u>why</u> did you come to the UK?

c) 怎么 zěnme

i) 'how'

你怎么去学校？
nǐ <u>zěnme</u> qù xuéxiào?
<u>how</u> do you get to school?

ii) 'why', 'how come' or 'how is it that'

他怎么知道？	你怎么不去？
tā <u>zěnme</u> zhīdào?	nǐ <u>zěnme</u> bú qù?
<u>how is it</u> that he knows?	<u>how come</u> you aren't going?

你怎么去了？
nǐ <u>zěnme</u> qù le?
<u>why</u> did you go?

d) 怎么样 zěnmeyàng (how)

i) asking for information:

最近怎么样？
zuìjìn <u>zěnmeyàng</u>?
<u>how</u> are you lately?

ii) when 怎么样 zěnmeyàng is preceded by the particle 得 de, it can be used to ask questions for which the response will usually indicate an extent, for example:

她的德文说得怎么样?

tāde Déwén shūo de zěnmeyàng?

<u>how</u>'s her spoken German?

iii) 怎么样 zěnmeyàng can also be used as an end tag, broadly meaning 'how about':

晚上出去吃饭, 怎么样?

wǎnshàng chūqù chīfàn, zěnmeyàng?

let's go out for a meal tonight, <u>what do you think</u>?

你跟她一起去, 怎么样?

nǐ gēn tā yìqǐ qù, zěnmeyàng?

<u>how about</u> you go with her?

e) 多 duō + adjective can be used to express how far/big/heavy/tall/high/long *etc* something is:

这里到邮局多远?

zhèlǐ dào yóujú <u>duō yuǎn</u>?

<u>how far</u> is the post office from here?

你的脚多大?

nǐde jiǎo <u>duō dà</u>?

<u>how big</u> are your feet?

这些香蕉多重?

zhèxiē xiāngjiāo <u>duō zhòng</u>?

<u>how heavy</u> are these bananas?

你多高?

nǐ <u>duō gāo</u>?

<u>how tall</u> are you?

Note that 有 yǒu can be placed before 多 duō for emphasis:

你有多高?

nǐ <u>yǒu duō gāo</u>?

<u>how tall</u> *are* you?

f) 多 duō + adverb can be used to express how quickly/soon/fast/early *etc* something is:

你能多早来?

nǐ néng <u>duō zǎo</u> lái?

<u>how early</u> can you be here?

他跑得多快?

tā pǎo de <u>duō kuài</u>?

<u>how fast</u> can he run?

g) 多久 duō jiǔ and 多长时间 duō cháng shíjiān (how long):

你来多久了?　　　　　　　　　你来多长时间了?
nǐ lái duō jiǔ le?　　　　　　　　nǐ lái duō cháng shíjiān le?
how long have you been here?　　how long have you been here?

h) 多少 duōshǎo (how much, how many):

　　i) 多少 duōshǎo + noun:

　　　　这个多少钱?
　　　　zhè ge duōshǎo qián?
　　　　how much (money) is this?

　　　　这里一共有多少学生?
　　　　zhèlǐ yígòng yǒu duōshǎo xuéshēng?
　　　　how many students are here altogether?

　　ii) 多少 duōshǎo + period of time:

　　　　多少天?　　　　　　　　多少年?
　　　　duōshǎo tiān?　　　　　duōshǎo nián?
　　　　how many days?　　　　how many years?

　　　　Note that it is necessary to include the measure word 个 ge
　　　　when using 多少 duōshǎo with the following expressions of
　　　　time: 钟头 zhōngtou and 小时 xiǎoshí (hour), 星期 xīngqī
　　　　(week), 月 yuè (month).

　　　　多少个月?　　　　　　　多少个星期?
　　　　duōshǎo ge yuè?　　　　duōshǎo ge xīngqī?
　　　　how many months?　　　how many weeks?

　　　　多少个钟头/小时?
　　　　duōshǎo ge zhōngtou/xiǎoshí?
　　　　how many hours?

i) 几 jǐ (how many) is only used to ask a question when the
anticipated answer is below ten. It is generally used in the
construction '几 jǐ + measure word + noun'.

你有几个孩子?
nǐ yǒu jǐ ge háizi?
how many children do you have?

这个房子有几个房间?

zhè ge fángzi yǒu jǐ ge fángjiān?

<u>how many</u> rooms are there in this house?

从这里到伦敦要几个小时?

cóng zhèlǐ dào Lúndūn yào jǐ ge xiǎoshí?

<u>how many</u> hours is it from here to London?

几 jǐ can also be used to ask about times and dates. Note that no measure word is needed in this case:

几点?   几月几日?

jǐ diǎn?   jǐ yuè jǐ rì?

<u>what</u>'s the time?   (*lit.* <u>what</u> month <u>what</u> day?)

                                          what's the date?

3 Choice-type questions

Questions that offer the listener a choice between two or more alternatives can be formed by inserting the linking word 还是 háishì (or) between the two options:

你要茶还是咖啡?

nǐ yào chá háishì kāfēi?

would you like tea <u>or</u> coffee (<u>or both</u>)?

If strictly one option only can be selected, the particle 呢 ne must be inserted at the end of the question:

你要茶还是咖啡呢?

nǐ yào chá háishì kāfēi <u>ne</u>?

would you like tea <u>or</u> coffee?

Note that 还是 háishì is generally only used when forming questions. To express 'or' in statements 或(者) huò(zhě) (or, either ... or) is used:

你喜欢游泳还是跑步?

nǐ xǐhuān yóuyǒng <u>háishì</u> pǎobù?

do you prefer swimming <u>or</u> jogging?

游泳或者跑步, 我都喜欢

yóuyǒng <u>huòzhě</u> pǎobù, wǒ dōu xǐhuān

<u>either</u> (swimming <u>or</u> jogging), I like them both

The form 或者 huòzhě is generally used in spoken Chinese, whereas its abbreviated form 或 huò is used more formally and in written Chinese.

4 The construction 是 shì ... 的 de

a) The construction 是 shì ... 的 de is often used with question words to highlight the time, place, methods, aims *etc* of an action in the past ('when did ...', 'where did ...' *etc*). For example:

他是什么时候去的?
tā shì shénme shíhòu qù de?
<u>when did</u> he leave?

他是怎么去的?
tā shì zěnme qù de?
<u>how did</u> he travel?

Note that in speech, 是 shì may be omitted:

他什么时候去的?
tā shénme shíhòu qù de?
<u>when did</u> he leave?

b) The particle 的 de is an important indicator of past actions. Questions can be also be formulated with 是 shì and without 的 de to emphasize present or future actions. Again, 是 shì is optional in speech.

他(是)什么时候去?
tā (shì) shénme shíhòu qù?
<u>when will</u> he be leaving?

他(是)怎么去?
tā (shì) zěnme qù?
<u>how will</u> he be travelling?

5 Question particles

In Chinese, the question particles 呢 ne, 吧 ba and 啊 a can be used to form questions in many different ways.

a) 呢 ne

   i) The particle 呢 ne can be used to form a question when the context is already known, or to turn a response into another question, similar to 'and you?' or 'how about ...?' in English. It appears after the noun or pronoun to which it refers.

很好，你呢？

hěn hǎo, nǐ <u>ne</u>?

very well, <u>and you</u>?

今天会刮风，明天呢？

jīntiān huì guāfēng, míngtiān <u>ne</u>?

it'll be windy today, <u>how about tomorrow</u>?

ii) 呢 ne can be used as a reinforcing end tag:

他不去，你呢？

tā bú qù, nǐ <u>ne</u>?

he's not going, <u>are you</u>?

iii) 呢 ne can be used to raise a question following a discussion, similar to 'but what if ... ?' in English:

他明天没来呢？　　　　　房间太小呢？

tā míngtiān méi lái <u>ne</u>?　　fángjiān tài xiǎo <u>ne</u>?

<u>what if</u> he isn't here tomorrow?　<u>what if</u> the room is too small?

b) 吧 ba

吧 ba may be added to the end of a statement to form a question. It corresponds roughly to the English 'you will ... won't you?' construction:

你明天去吧？

nǐ míngtiān qù <u>ba</u>?

you will go tomorrow, <u>won't you</u>?

Note that 吧 ba can also be used with a negative statement, for example:

你不是学生吧？

nǐ búshì xuéshēng <u>ba</u>?

you aren't a student, <u>are you</u>?

c) 啊 a

The particle 啊 a is similar to 'eh' or 'huh' in English and expresses uncertainty. For example, it can be used in a choice-type question to check or clarify a response. *See also* **pages 70–1**.

你跳舞还是打太极啊?

nǐ tiàowǔ háishì dǎ tàijí a?

are you dancing or practising tai chi, <u>eh</u>?

6 Rhetorical questions

a) The verb 是 shì (to be) and the question particle 吗 ma can be combined to create a rhetorical question:

他是中国人, 是吗?

tā shì Zhōngguó rén, <u>shì ma</u>?

he's Chinese, <u>is he</u>? *(it's a possibility but I'm not certain)*

To create a negative rhetorical question, the negator 不 bú must be added:

他是中国人, 不是吗?

tā shì Zhōngguó rén, <u>búshì ma</u>?

he's Chinese, <u>isn't he</u>? *(I believe he is Chinese)*

b) The adverb 难道 nándào can be used to express the speaker's shock, surprise or doubt. Note that the use of the question particle 吗 ma is optional in this case:

他是中国人, 难道你不知道(吗)?

tā shì Zhōngguó rén, <u>nándào</u> nǐ bù zhīdào (<u>ma</u>)?

he's Chinese, didn't you know?

大家都来, 难道你不来(吗)?

dàjiā dōu lái, <u>nándào</u> nǐ bù lái (<u>ma</u>)?

everyone's here, aren't you coming?

7 Tag questions

There are some typical tag question constructions that can be added to the end of a statement in Chinese to clarify whether an action is acceptable to the listener or not. These function in much the same way as their English equivalents:

好吗 hǎo ma	OK
行吗 xíng ma	all right
可以吗 kěyǐ ma	is it possible
你说呢 nǐ shuō ne	what do you think

我们下星期去, 好吗?
wǒmen xià xīngqī qù, <u>hǎo ma</u>?
we'll go next week, <u>OK</u>?

我现在吃午饭, 可以吗?
wǒ xiànzài chī wǔfàn, <u>kěyǐ ma</u>?
I'm having my lunch now, <u>if I may</u>?

我们先吃晚饭再去, 你说呢?
wǒmen xiān chī wǎnfàn zài qù, <u>nǐ shuō ne</u>?
we'll have dinner before we go, <u>what do you think</u>?

我出去一下, 行吗?
wǒ chūqù yíxià, <u>xíng ma</u>?
I'm popping outside, <u>all right</u>?

5 NOUNS

A noun is a word or group of words that refers to a person, an animal, a thing, a place or an abstract idea.

 A COMMON NOUNS

Common nouns refer to general items or ideas, as opposed to proper nouns (*see pages 42-3*) which are the names of particular people, places and things.

1 Singular and plural

There is no distinction between singular and plural common nouns in Chinese.

学生	桌子	公园
xuésheng	zhuōzi	gōngyuán
student/students	table/tables	park/parks

However, when a common noun is used with a numeral, a measure word must be inserted between the numeral and the noun. *For more on measure words see* **pages 124-8.**

Numeral	Measure word	Noun	Meaning
一 yí	个 gè	学生 xuésheng	a/one student
三 sān	个 gè	公园 gōngyuán	three parks
五 wǔ	个 gè	桌子 zhuōzi	five tables

2 Human nouns

Common nouns referring to people, also known as 'human nouns',
may be pluralized by adding the suffix 们 men.

a) A human noun with the 们 men suffix becomes definite:

学生们已经走了　　　　　　　　孩子们都笑了
xuéshengmen yǐjīng zǒu le　　　háizimen dōu xiào le
the students had left　　　　　all the children laughed

However, the word 人们 rénmen refers to 'people' in an indefinite
sense. For example, 人们说 rénmen shuō can be translated as
'people say' or 'they say'.

b) A noun ending in the suffix 们 men cannot be used with a
measure word, as the suffix alone indicates that the noun is
plural:

七个学生　　　　　　*never*　　　　　七个学生们
qī gè xuéshēng　　　　　　　　　　　qī gè xuéshēngmen
seven students

c) 们 men is never used with non-human nouns:

那些小猫　　　　　　*never*　　　　　那些小猫们
nàxiē xiǎo māo　　　　　　　　　　　nàxiē xiǎo māomen
those cats

很多桌子　　　　　　*never*　　　　　很多桌子们
hěn duō zhuōzi　　　　　　　　　　　hěn duō zhuōzimen
many tables

B PROPER NOUNS

A proper noun is the name for a particular person, place or
thing. In English, proper nouns always begin with a capital letter
regardless of where they occur in a sentence. In Chinese, however,
as it is impossible to capitalize Chinese characters, this distinction

does not occur. Note, however, that in pinyin the initial letter is capitalized.

Names of people are written with the surname first, the given name second and the title third (when used):

成龙	李小龙	周杰伦
Chéng Lóng	Lǐ Xiǎolóng	Zhōu Jié Lún
Jackie Chan	Bruce Lee	Jay Chou
章子怡	刘玉玲	
Zhāng Zǐyí	Liú Yùlíng	
Ziyi Zhang	Lucy Liu	

 C NOUN PHRASES

The noun is usually the last part of a noun phrase. Adjectives, including numerals, generally occur *in front* of the nouns they describe, as in English:

一只狗	这个学校	暖和的春天
yì zhī gǒu	zhè ge xuéxiào	nuǎnhé de chūntiān
a/one dog	this school	warm spring

The particle 的 de can be placed in front of a noun to indicate that it is the main noun described:

他买的笔很漂亮
tā mǎi de bǐ hěn piàoliàng
(*lit.* he bought pen very beautiful)
the pen he bought is very beautiful

妈妈做的饭最好吃
Māma zuò de fàn zuì hǎochī
(*lit.* Mum prepared meal most delicious)
the meal prepared by Mum is most delicious

我不认识他旁边的女孩

wǒ bú rènshì <u>tā pángbiān de</u> nǚhái

(*lit.* I don't know <u>beside him</u> girl)

I don't know <u>the girl who is beside him</u>

说话的人们

shuōhuà <u>de rénmen</u>

(*lit.* talking <u>people</u>)

<u>the people</u> who are talking

6 PRONOUNS

For a list of interrogative pronouns, see **pages 30-2**.

A PERSONAL PRONOUNS

Personal pronouns refer to people or things ('I, you, he, she, it' etc). In Chinese there is no distinction between personal pronouns as the subject of the sentence (eg 'I, we') and personal pronouns as the object (eg 'me, us').

1 Singular

1st person	我 wǒ	I/me
2nd person	你 nǐ	you
	您 nín	you *(respectful)*
3rd person	他 tā	he/him
	她 tā	she/her
	它 tā	it

Note that there is no difference between the 3rd person singular forms in spoken Chinese or pinyin, but that in written Chinese different forms of the characters are used.

我不认识他
wǒ bú rènshì tā
I don't know him

他喜欢她
tā xǐhuān tā
he likes her

您是苏格兰人吗?
nín shì Sūgélán rén ma?
are you Scottish?

他给我一本书
tā gěi wǒ yì běn shù
he gave me a book

请别动它!
qǐng bié dòng tā!
please don't touch it!

2 Plural

Plural pronouns are formed using the singular pronouns and the pluralizer suffix 们 men. *See also* page 42.

1st person	我们 wǒmen	we/us
	咱们 zánmen	we/us

There are two forms of the 1st person plural:

我们 wǒmen is listener-exclusive, ie 'we, may or may not include you'.

咱们 zánmen is listener-inclusive, ie 'we, including you'.

我们去看电影
<u>wǒmen</u> qù kàndiànyǐng
<u>we</u>'re off to the movies

咱们去看电影
<u>zánmen</u> qù kàndiànyǐng
<u>let's</u> go to the movies

2nd person	你们 nǐmen	you

你们是网球员吗?
<u>nǐmen</u> shì wǎngqiú yuán ma?
are <u>you</u> tennis players?

Note that 您 nín (the respectful form of 'you') has no plural form. To talk about more than one person respectfully, it is necessary to use the 'numeral + measure word + noun' construction:

您两位是新老师吗?
<u>nín</u> liǎng wèi shì xīn lǎoshī ma?
are <u>you</u> two the new teachers?

3rd person	他们 tāmen	they/them *(m/mixed)*
	她们 tāmen	they/them *(f)*
	它们 tāmen	they/them

他们喜欢游泳
<u>tāmen</u> xǐhuān yóuyǒng
<u>they</u> like swimming *(m)*

她们住在伦敦
<u>tāmen</u> zhù zài Lúndūn
<u>they</u> live in London *(f)*

它 tā (it) and 它们 tāmen (they, them) are mostly used to refer to living things, such as animals, rather than inanimate objects.

它们不是我的狗，是我朋友的
<u>tāmen</u> bú shì wǒde gǒu, shì wǒ péngyǒude
<u>they</u>'re not my dogs, they belong to my friend

园子里有很多蚊子，它们真讨厌！
yuánzi lǐ yǒu hěn duō wénzi, <u>tāmen</u> zhēn tǎoyàn!
there are a lot of mosquitoes in the garden, <u>they</u>'re really nasty!

B THE REFLEXIVE PRONOUN 自己 ZÌJǏ

Reflexive pronouns in English are words like 'myself', 'yourself' *etc.* In Chinese, these are all expressed with one pronoun, 自己 zìjǐ.

1 Personal pronoun + 自己 zìjǐ

她自己坐公车上学
<u>tā zìjǐ</u> zuò gōngchē shàngxué
<u>she</u> takes the bus to school by <u>herself</u>

我们自己走了
<u>wǒmen zìjǐ</u> zǒu le
<u>we</u> left by <u>ourselves</u>

别怪你自己
bié guài <u>nǐ zìjǐ</u>
don't blame <u>yourself</u>

你自己来
<u>nǐ zìjǐ</u> lái
do it <u>yourself</u>

Note that when the same personal pronoun appears twice in a sentence with the reflexive, it can be omitted in either the first or second part of the sentence. For example:

这件事(我)只能怪我自己
zhè jiàn shì (<u>wǒ</u>) zhǐ néng guài <u>wǒ zìjǐ</u>
(*lit.* this matter [I] can only blame <u>myself</u>)
I can only blame myself in this matter

这件事我只能怪(我)自己
zhè jiàn shì wǒ zhǐ néng guài (wǒ) zìjǐ
(*lit.* this matter I can only blame [myself])
I can only blame myself in this matter

2 Personal pronoun + 自己 **zìjǐ** +的 **de** ('my own, your own' *etc*)

这是你自己的事
zhè shì nǐ zìjǐde shì
that's <u>your own</u> business

你们自己的书，要记得带回家
nǐmen zìjǐde shū, yào jìdé dài huíjiā
remember to take <u>your own</u> book home with you

Note that the particle 的de *never* occurs between a personal
pronoun and the reflexive pronoun 自己 zìjǐ.

C POSSESSIVE PRONOUNS

Possessive pronouns consist of a personal pronoun + 的 de. Chinese
does not distinguish between possessive adjectives (eg 'my') and
possessive pronouns (eg 'mine').

1 Singular

我的 wǒde	my/mine
你的 nǐde	your/yours
您的 nínde	your/yours *(respectful)*
他的 tāde	his
她的 tāde	her/hers
它的 tāde	its

2 Plural

我们的 wǒmende	our/ours
咱们的 zánmende	our/ours
你们的 nǐmende	your/yours
他们的 tāmende	their/theirs
她们的 tāmende	their/theirs
它们的 tāmende	their/theirs

3 Optional 的 de

The particle 的 de is optional when talking about something
familiar, such as:

a) People close to you, eg family members, friends, work
colleagues, classmates *etc*:

我(的)爸爸	我(的)同学	她(的)好朋友
<u>wǒ (de)</u> bàba	<u>wǒ (de)</u> tóngxué	<u>tā (de)</u> hǎo péngyǒu
<u>my</u> father	<u>my</u> classmate	<u>her</u> good friend

b) A place closely connected to you, eg home, school, country *etc*:

她(的)家在这里	我们(的)国家	你(的)学校
<u>tā (de)</u> jiā zài zhèlǐ	<u>wǒmen (de)</u> guójiā	<u>nǐ (de)</u> xuéxiào
<u>her</u> home is here	<u>our</u> country	<u>your</u> school

D RELATIVE PRONOUNS

Relative pronouns (eg 'who, whom, whose, which' and 'that')
are used in English to refer back to people or things previously
mentioned, but there are no equivalents in Chinese. The following
examples illustrate how the particle 的 de is used in place of a

relative pronoun to link a noun phrase to a relative clause. The particle 的 de occurs before the main noun:

进来的那个男孩是我哥哥
jìnlái de nà ge nánhái shì wǒ gēge
(*lit.* came in <u>who</u> the boy is my elder brother)
the boy who came in is my elder brother

你见过的那个女孩 是一位天才
nǐ jiàn-guò de nà ge nǚhái shì yí wèi tiāncái
the girl <u>whom</u> you have met is a genius

借你球拍的男孩
jiè nǐ qiúpāi de nánhái
the boy <u>whose</u> racquet you borrowed

你正在看的这个节目 是我最喜欢的
nǐ zhèngzài kàn de zhè ge jiémù shì wǒ zuì xǐhuān de
the programme <u>which</u> you are watching is my favourite

你来的那一天 是我的生日
nǐ lái de nà yì tiān shì wǒde shēngrì
the day <u>that</u> you came was my birthday

 E DEMONSTRATIVE PRONOUNS

Demonstrative pronouns are used to refer to a specific person or thing. The main demonstrative pronouns in Chinese are:

这 zhè	this
那 nà	that
这些 zhèxiē	these
那些 nàxiē	those

这些比那些贵
<u>zhèxiē</u> bǐ <u>nàxiē</u> guì
<u>these</u> (ones) are more expensive than <u>those</u> (ones)

Note that 这 zhè (this) and 那 nà (that) must be followed by the appropriate measure word when used as demonstrative adjectives (*see* pages 124–8):

这个演员
zhè ge yǎnyuán
<u>this</u> actor

这辆车
zhè liàng chē
<u>this</u> car

那个漂亮的女生
<u>nà ge</u> piàoliàng de nǚshēng
<u>that</u> pretty girl

我比较喜欢那个
wǒ bǐjiào xǐhuān <u>nà ge</u>
I prefer <u>that one</u>

7 ADJECTIVES

Adjectives are words used to describe or give more information about nouns.

A ATTRIBUTIVE ADJECTIVES

An attributive adjective is one that directly modifies the noun. In Chinese, just as in English, the adjective comes immediately before the noun:

男学生	红花	黑裤子
nán xuésheng	hóng huā	hēi kùzi
<u>male</u> student	<u>red</u> flower	<u>black</u> trousers
热汤	小房子	大书包
rè tāng	xiǎo fángzi	dà shūbao
<u>hot</u> soup	<u>small</u> house	<u>big</u> schoolbag

1 The particle 的 de

When an adjective is composed of more than one character, the particle 的 de must be inserted between the adjective and the noun:

可爱的猫	好看的衣服	简单的歌
kě'ài de māo	hǎokàn de yīfú	jiǎndān de gē
<u>cute</u> cat	<u>nice</u> clothes	<u>simple</u> song
简单的问题	善良的人	
jiǎndān de wèntí	shànliáng de rén	
<u>simple</u> question	<u>kind-hearted</u> person	

2 Adverb + adjective

Adverbs of degree (words such as 'very', 'extremely' *etc*) usually come before the adjective they are modifying:

很贵	最贵	太贵
hěn guì	zuì guì	tài guì
<u>very</u> expensive	<u>most</u> expensive	<u>too</u> expensive

B ADJECTIVAL STATIVE VERBS

1 General points

Some adjectives in Chinese can also function as verbs. Nevertheless, they are translated as adjectives, not verbs, in English and are therefore sometimes known as adjectival stative verbs.

Adjectival stative verbs in Chinese are equivalent to predicative adjectives in English. A predicative adjective is one that comes after the noun and is joined to it by a linking verb, often the verb 'to be', for example 'my food **was** very **spicy**', 'that girl **is** pretty'.

In Chinese, adjectives used in this way do not require a linking verb (for example 是 shì 'to be'), instead they function as both the verb and the adjective:

我很好
wǒ hěn hǎo
(*lit.* I very <u>good</u>)
I <u>am well</u>

这个菜真辣
zhè gè cài zhēn <u>là</u>
(*lit.* this dish really <u>spicy</u>)
this dish <u>is</u> really <u>spicy</u>

我哥哥很高
wǒ gēge hěn <u>gāo</u>
(*lit.* my brother very <u>tall</u>)
my brother <u>is</u> very <u>tall</u>

Note that the verb 是 shì (to be) is occasionally used to add emphasis to a statement. For example:

我哥哥是很高
wǒ gēge <u>shì</u> hěn gāo
my brother <u>is</u> very tall *(I told you so)*

这个菜是辣!
zhè gè cài <u>shì</u> là!
this dish <u>is</u> spicy! *(surprise)*

> *Note*
>
> The verb 是 shì (to be) must be used when linking a subject noun with another noun or pronoun, for example when describing a profession, identity or nationality. *For this use see* page 74.

2 Negation

不 bù is placed before the adjectival stative verb to negate it. For example:

我不忙
wǒ <u>bù</u> máng
(lit. I <u>not</u> busy)
I'm not busy

学中文不难
xué Zhōngwén <u>bù nán</u>
(lit. learn Chinese <u>not difficult</u>)
it's <u>not difficult</u> to learn Chinese

Note that 不 bú 'not' and 够 gòu 'enough' must always appear in that order:

他的英语不够好
tāde Yīngyǔ <u>bú gòu hǎo</u>
(lit. his English <u>not enough good</u>)
his English <u>isn't good enough</u>

这个房间不够大
zhè gè fángjiān <u>bú gòu dà</u>
(lit. this room <u>not enough big</u>)
this room <u>isn't big enough</u>

3 Forming questions

See also pages 28–40.

There are two ways to form questions with adjectival stative verbs:

- ❏ with the construction 'adjectival stative verb + 吗 ma'
- ❏ with the question form 'adjectival stative verb + 不 bù + adjectival stative verb'

中文难吗?	你高兴不高兴?
zhōngwén <u>nán ma</u>?	nǐ <u>gāoxìng bù gāoxing</u>?
<u>is</u> Chinese <u>difficult</u>?	(*lit.* you <u>happy not happy</u>?)
	are you happy?

8 ADVERBS

Adverbs are words used to provide additional information about other parts of speech, including verbs, adjectives and other adverbs. In Chinese, they are used especially to indicate notions such as degree, time, duration and frequency, approximation, possibility, affirmation or negation and tone.

They may be divided into different types, as outlined below.

 A TYPES OF ADVERB

1 Adverbs of degree

This is the most common type of adverb. Adverbs of degree refer to the intensity of an action or the degree to which something is true and appear before an adjective or another adverb:

很 hěn	very
太 tài	too
真 zhēn	really
更 gèng	even more
非常 fēicháng	extremely, terribly
十分 shífēn	extremely
特别 tèbié	exceptionally
多么 duōme	how, so

这些花长得很快
zhèxiē huā zhǎng-de <u>hěn</u> kuài
these flowers grow <u>very</u> quickly

她真漂亮
tā <u>zhēn</u> piàoliang
she is <u>really</u> beautiful

你说得太快了
nǐ shuō-de <u>tài</u> kuài le
you spoke <u>too</u> quickly

她更漂亮了
tā <u>gèng</u> piàoliang le
she is becoming <u>even more</u> beautiful

他说的话非常重要
tā shuō de huà fēicháng zhòngyào
what he said is <u>extremely</u> important

我十分满意
wǒ shífēn mǎnyì
I am <u>extremely</u> satisfied

这幅画特别好
zhè fú huà tèbié hǎo
this painting is <u>exceptionally</u> good

我非常抱歉
wǒ fēicháng bàoqiàn
I'm <u>terribly</u> sorry

宇宙是多么广阔啊！
yǔzhòu <u>duōme</u> guǎngkuò a!
the universe is <u>so</u> vast!

看，这小狗多么聪明！
kàn, zhè xiǎogǒu <u>duōme</u> cōngmíng!
look <u>how</u> clever this dog is!

2 Adverbs of scope

These adverbs appear before a verb and are generally used to indicate scope or range:

都 dōu	all
全 quán	all
只 zhǐ	only
一共 yígòng	altogether
一起 yìqǐ	together

他们都来了
tāmen <u>dōu</u> lái le
they <u>all</u> came

她只有一本中文书
tā <u>zhǐ</u> yǒu yì běn Zhōngwén shū
she has <u>only</u> one Chinese book

我们全会说法语
wǒmen <u>quán</u> huì shuō Fǎyǔ
we can <u>all</u> speak French

昨天他们一起去吃饭
zuótiān tāmen <u>yìqǐ</u> qù chīfàn
yesterday they had a meal <u>together</u>

这里一共有八个人
zhèlǐ <u>yígòng</u> yǒu bā ge rén
there are eight people here <u>altogether</u>

3 Adverbs of time and duration

In general, these refer to when or over what length of time
something occurs:

已经 yǐjīng	already
正在 zhèngzài	now
刚 gāng	just
就 jiù	right away; as early as
一直 yìzhí	always
仍然 réngrán	still *(continuing now)*
还 hái	still *(up to this time)*

她已经走了
tā yǐjīng zǒu le
she has <u>already</u> left

我刚听到了一个消息
wǒ <u>gāng</u> tīngdào le yí ge xiāoxi
I have <u>just</u> heard the good news

我去年就毕业了
wǒ qù nián <u>jiù</u> bìyè le
I graduated <u>as early as</u> last year

妈妈正在客厅休息
māma <u>zhèngzài</u> kètīng xiūxi
Mum is <u>now</u> in the lounge resting

他就来
tā <u>jiù</u> lai
he will come <u>right away</u>

她一直住在北京
tā <u>yìzhí</u> zhù zài Běijīng
she has <u>always</u> lived in Beijing

和你聊了一天，我仍然不知道你的名字
hé nǐ liáo-le yì tiān, wǒ <u>réngrán</u> bù zhīdào nǐde míngzi
I've chatted to you all day and I <u>still</u> don't know your name

我还有时间赶最后一趟车
wǒ <u>hái</u> yǒu shíjiān gǎn zuìhòu yítàng chē
I <u>still</u> have time to catch the last bus

4 Adverbs of doubt and certainty

These adverbs are used to express degrees of certainty or possibility.

a) expressing doubt

大概 dàgài	probably, most likely
也许 yěxǔ	maybe, perhaps; probably
或许 huòxǔ	maybe, perhaps; probably
可能 kěnéng	possibly

他今天大概生病了
tā jīntiān dàgài shēngbìng le
he is <u>probably</u> ill today

我明天大概还会来
wǒ míngtiān dàgài hái huì lái
I shall <u>very likely</u> be here again tomorrow

他今天也许生病了
tā jīntiān yěxǔ shēngbìng le
he is <u>probably</u> ill today

这或许是他的书包
zhè huòxǔ shì tāde shūbāo
this is <u>probably</u> his bag

他也许是错的
tā yěxǔ shì cuò de
<u>perhaps</u> he is wrong

他可能是日本人
tā kěnéng shì Rìběn rén
he is <u>possibly</u> Japanese

b) expressing certainty

肯定 kěndìng	certainly
一定 yídìng	definitely
必定 bìdìng	undoubtedly, surely

我肯定能按时完成工作
wǒ kěndìng néng ànshí wánchéng gōngzuò
I can <u>certainly</u> have the job finished on time

八点以前，我一定回家
bā diǎn yǐqián, wǒ yídìng huíjiā
I shall <u>definitely</u> be home before eight o'clock

我相信只要尽最大努力，必定会成功

wǒ xiāngxìn zhǐyào jìn zuì dà nǔlì, <u>bìdìng</u> huì chénggōng

I believe that if I do my utmost, I will <u>surely</u> succeed

Note that 肯定 kěndìng, 一定 yídìng and 必定 bìdìng are very similar. However, 必定 bìdìng tends to be used mainly in advertising slogans or inspirational phrases.

5 Adverbs of frequency

These are used to refer to how often something happens:

总是 zǒngshì	always
老是 lǎoshì	always
常(常) cháng(cháng)	frequently
经常 jīngcháng	regularly
很少 hěn shǎo	hardly, rarely
又 yòu	again (*action in the past*)
再 zài	again (*action yet to take place*)
从来没 cónglái méi	never

他总是迟到

tā zǒngshì chídào

he is <u>always</u> late

他老是烦我

tā lǎoshì fán wǒ

he is <u>always</u> pestering me

小李常(常)给我写信

Xiǎo Lǐ <u>cháng(cháng)</u> gěi wǒ xiěxìn

Xiao Li <u>frequently</u> writes to me

奶奶经常到公园打太极拳

nǎinai <u>jīngcháng</u> dào gōngyuán dǎ tàijíquán

Granny <u>regularly</u> goes to the park to practise tai chi

这儿很少下雨

zhèr <u>hěn shǎo</u> xiàyǔ

it <u>hardly</u> rains here

我们明天再说吧！

wǒmen míngtiān <u>zài</u> shuō ba!

we'll speak <u>again</u> tomorrow

那个电影，我昨天又去看了
nàge diànyǐng, wǒ zuótiān yòu qù kàn le
I watched that movie <u>again</u> yesterday

我从来没去过长城
wǒ cónglái méi qù-guò Chángchéng
I've <u>never</u> been to the Great Wall

Note that 从来没 cónglái méi is typically placed before the construction 'verb + aspect marker 过 guò' to mean 'never (done something) before'.

6 Adverbs of evaluation and viewpoint

These adverbs are used to describe or emphasize the attitude, emotions or point of view of the speaker:

究竟 jiūjìng	actually
到底 dàodǐ	after all
都 dōu	already
才 cái	really
就 jiù	simply

你究竟爱不爱她？
nǐ jiūjìng ài bú ài tā?
do you <u>actually</u> love her?

我到底还是个初学者
wǒ dàodǐ háishì ge chūxuézhě
<u>after all</u>, I'm still just a beginner

都中午十二点了，你还睡觉！
dōu zhōngwǔ shí-èr diǎn le, nǐ hái shuìjiào!
it's <u>already</u> midday and you are still in bed!

她才不原谅你呢！
tā cái bú yuánliàng nǐ ne!
she <u>really</u> doesn't want to forgive you!

我就不告诉你！
wǒ jiù bú gàosù nǐ!
I <u>simply</u> don't want to tell you!

B POSITION OF THE ADVERB

In Chinese, the position of the adverb in the sentence can vary. The adverb typically occurs:

❑ after the subject noun, for example:

> 他们都去学校了
> tāmen <u>dōu</u> qù xuéxiào le
> they've <u>all</u> gone to school

❑ before a verb, adjective or another adverb, for example:

> 天又下雨了
> tiān <u>yòu</u> xiàyǔ le
> it's raining <u>again</u>

❑ before a modal verb, for example:

> 我觉得我们都应该去
> wǒ juéde wǒmen <u>dōu</u> yīnggāi qù
> I think we should <u>all</u> go

❑ before a negator for example:

> 我觉得我们都不应该去
> wǒ juéde wǒmen <u>dōu</u> bù yīnggāi qù
> I don't think we should <u>all</u> go

> ## Note
>
> 也许 yěxǔ (maybe, perhaps) and 到底 dàodǐ (after all) can be placed before *or* after the subject noun:
>
> 她也许去游泳了
> tā <u>yěxǔ</u> qù yóuyǒng le
> <u>maybe</u> she's gone swimming
>
> 你到底懂不懂？
> nǐ <u>dàodǐ</u> dǒng bù dǒng?
> do you understand <u>after all</u>?
>
> 也许她去游泳了
> <u>yěxǔ</u> tā qù yóuyǒng le
> <u>maybe</u> she's gone swimming
>
> 到底你懂不懂？
> <u>dàodǐ</u> nǐ dǒng bù dǒng?
> do you understand <u>after all</u>?

 MODIFYING ADJECTIVES

In Chinese, the adverbial particle 地 dì is often inserted immediately after the adjective to create an adverb. This is similar to the way that the suffix '-ly' is added to many English adjectives to form adverbs, eg 'loud–loudly'.

她慢慢地写 tā <u>mànmandi</u> xiě she wrote <u>slowly</u>	哥哥轻轻地走 gēge <u>qīngqingdi</u> zǒu (my/his *etc*) older brother walked <u>quietly</u>

妹妹安静地吃
mèimei <u>ānjìngdi</u> chī
(my/his *etc*) younger sister ate
   <u>quietly</u>
	他小心地走过那条窄桥
	tā <u>xiǎoxīndi</u> zǒu guò nàtiáo zhǎi
	   qiáo
	he walked <u>carefully</u> across the
	   narrow bridge

SOME PARTICULAR CASES

The following adverbs are worthy of particular note because they:

- are very frequent in everyday language
- often have more than one meaning
- are known to be especially difficult for learners of Chinese

1 都 **dōu**

a) Used on its own, the adverb 都 dōu can have the following meanings:

all, both

什么都行 shénme <u>dōu</u> xíng <u>anything</u> will do	他们都到了 tāmen <u>dōu</u> dào le they are <u>both/all</u> here

even
我都不知道
wǒ <u>dōu</u> bù zhīdào
I don't <u>even</u> know (about it)

anything
我都不知道
wǒ <u>dōu</u> bù zhīdào
I don't know <u>anything</u> about it

already
爷爷都过了八十八岁
yéye <u>dōu</u> guò le bā shí bā suì
Grandpa's <u>already</u> eighty-eight years old

b) 都 dōu is often used in the sense of 'all' before 是 shì (to be) to indicate the cause of something:

都是你的错
<u>dōu shì</u> nǐde cuò
<u>it's all</u> your fault

都是你调皮，我们也被罚了
<u>dōu shì</u> nǐ tiáopí, wǒmen yě bèi fá le
<u>it's all because of</u> your naughtiness that we were punished

c) 都 dōu is combined with 也 yě (too) to give 也都 yě dōu, which means 'and ... too':

明年我们都去中国，他们也都去中国
míngnián wǒmen dōu qù Zhōngguó, tāmen <u>yě dōu</u> qù Zhōngguó
next year we'll be going to China, <u>and</u> they'll be going <u>too</u>

我们喜欢吃面，也都喜欢吃汉堡包
wǒmen xǐhuān chī miàn, <u>yě dōu</u> xǐhuān chī hànbǎobāo
we like noodles <u>and</u> hamburgers <u>too</u>

2 就 jiù

The adverb 就 jiù can have several different meanings:

right away, immediately

我就来

wǒ jiù lái

I'll come <u>right away</u>

as soon as, right after

她一见到我就笑了

tā yí jiàndào wǒ jiù xiào le

<u>as soon as</u> she saw me, she smiled

then, in that case

如果你有时间和我谈一谈，我就开心了

rúguǒ nǐ yǒu shíjiān hé wǒ tán-yì-tán, wǒ jiù kāixīn le

if you've time to talk to me, <u>then</u> I'm happy

simply, just

我就不喜欢他

wǒ jiù bù xǐhuān tā

I <u>simply</u> don't like him

他就喜欢打网球

tā jiù xǐhuān dǎ wǎngqiú

he <u>just</u> likes to play tennis

only, just, merely

就有一条大号的牛仔裤

jiù yǒu yìtiáo dàhào de niúzǎikù

there is <u>only</u> one large pair of jeans

exactly, precisely

这就是我要的书

zhè jiù shì wǒ yào de shū

this is <u>precisely</u> the book I wanted

even if

我就不说，他也知道

wǒ jiù bù shuō, tā yě zhīdào

<u>even if</u> I don't tell, he'll still know

3 才 cái

The adverb 才 cái means 'only', 'not until' or 'unless' and can be used with various other expressions:

a) 才 cái can be used with an expression of time, for example:

他七点钟才到
tā qī diǎnzhōng <u>cái</u> dào
he is <u>not</u> coming <u>until</u> 7 o'clock

b) 才 cái can be used with an expression of reason or condition to mean 'not unless', 'not until' or 'only when/then', for example:

你解释后，我才明白是怎么一回事
nǐ jiěshì hòu, wǒ <u>cái</u> míngbái shì zěnme yì huíshì
<u>only when</u> you explained it to me did I understand what was going on

c) 才 cái can be used with a numerical expression:

我才二十一岁
wǒ <u>cái</u> èr-shí-yī suì
I'm <u>only</u> 21 years old

d) 才 cái can be used emphatically with 呢 ne at the end of the sentence, to give the meaning 'actually':

我不好看，他才好看呢！
wǒ bù hǎokàn, tā <u>cái</u> hǎokàn ne!
I'm not the good-looking one, (<u>actually</u>) he is!

See page 116 *for more on the use of* 才 cái.

9 IMPERATIVES AND EXCLAMATIVES

A IMPERATIVES

Typically, the imperative is used to give commands, orders and instructions or to make polite requests or suggestions. Imperative sentences do not have a clear subject and should be used with care in order to avoid seeming impolite.

出来！	坐下！	吃饭！
chūlái!	zuòxià!	chīfàn!
come out!	sit down!	eat!

1 Polite imperatives

Instructions that are preceded by 请 qǐng (please) or followed by the particle 吧 ba are perceived as more polite:

请出来！
<u>qǐng</u> chūlái!
<u>please</u> come out!

出来吧！
chūlái <u>ba</u>!
come out <u>then</u>!

请坐！
<u>qǐng</u> zuò!
<u>please</u> sit down!

坐吧！
zuò <u>ba</u>!
<u>why don't you</u> take a seat!

When 请 qǐng occurs together with the particle 吧 ba, the imperative can carry a pleading tone:

请出来吧！
<u>qǐng</u> chūlái <u>ba</u>!
<u>won't you please</u> come out!

请吃饭吧！
<u>qǐng</u> chīfàn <u>ba</u>!
<u>won't you please</u> have something to eat!

2 Imperatives with an adverb

Imperatives may occur with an emphatic adverb, which is usually placed before the verb. This is used to make requests or give instructions, and allows the speaker to express how the actions are to be carried out:

快出来!	慢慢吃!
kuài chūlái!	mànman chī!
come out <u>quickly</u>!	eat <u>slowly</u>!

To soften the tone of imperatives with an adverb, 请 qǐng (please) can be placed at the start of the sentence. Alternatively, the particle 吧 ba can be added at the end of the sentence.

请快出来!	慢慢吃吧!
qǐng kuài chūlái!	mànman chī ba!
come out quickly, <u>please</u>!	eat slowly <u>then</u>!

3 Imperatives with 咱们 zánmen or 我们 wǒmen

When the function of the imperative is to make a suggestion that includes the speaker *and* the listener, the first person plural 咱们 zánmen or 我们 wǒmen can be omitted. In a way, this is similar to the English, whereby 'let us' is frequently contracted to 'let's'. For example:

(我们) 走吧!	(咱们) 明天再来!
(<u>wǒmen</u>) zǒu ba!	(<u>zánmen</u>) míngtiān zài lái!
<u>let's</u> go!	<u>let's</u> come again tomorrow!

4 Imperatives with 让 ràng or 叫 jiào

The third person imperative is formed by placing 让 ràng (to let, to allow) or 叫 jiào (to order) before a pronoun. It is most typically used to make requests or commands involving a third party. Broadly speaking, 叫 jiào is stronger and harsher in tone than 让 ràng.

让他明天给我打电话！
<u>ràng</u> tā míngtiān gěi wǒ dǎdiànhuà!
<u>let</u> him call me tomorrow!

叫他说！
<u>jiào</u> tā shuō!
<u>tell</u> him to speak!

When using 让 ràng or 叫 jiào, the speaker's agreement can be demonstrated by placing 吧 ba at the end of the sentence:

让他们去吧！
<u>ràng</u> tāmen qù <u>ba</u>!
<u>yes, let</u> them go!

5 Negative imperatives

a) In informal spoken language, negative imperatives are constructed with the negator 不要 búyào (do not). Its contracted form, 别 bié (don't), is the most common.

别出来！
<u>bié</u> chūlái!
<u>don't</u> come out!

别吃饭！
<u>bié</u> chīfàn!
<u>don't</u> eat!

不要出来！
<u>búyào</u> chūlái!
<u>do not</u> come out!

不要吃饭！
<u>búyào</u> chīfàn!
<u>do not</u> eat!

Sometimes, negative imperatives may contain the particle 了 le, which is used to indicate the desire to stop an action:

别吃饭了！
<u>bié</u> chīfàn <u>le</u>!
<u>stop</u> eating!

别睡觉了
<u>bié</u> shuìjiào <u>le</u>!
(*lit.* stop sleeping!)
wake up!

b) Negative imperatives with 不准 bùzhǔn (not allowed), 不许 bùxǔ (not permitted), 不得 bùdé (must not) and 禁止 jìnzhǐ (forbidden) are perceived as more formal:

不准停车！
<u>bù zhǔn</u> tíngchē!
<u>no</u> parking!

不得照相！
<u>bùdé</u> zhàoxiàng!
<u>no</u> photography!

禁止右转！
<u>jìnzhǐ</u> yòu zhuǎn!
<u>no</u> right turn!

 EXCLAMATIVES

Exclamative sentences are used to express a strong reaction, usually one of surprise or shock.

1 Exclamatives with 多么 duōme and 真 zhēn

Exclamatives formed with the adverbs 多么 duōme (how/such/what a ...!) and 真 zhēn (really) may be used to give a statement stronger emphasis. Generally, exclamatives with 多么 duōme cannot be used in the same clause as the adverb 很 hěn (very). Note that the inclusion of 么 me is optional:

你听，她唱得多(么)好听！
nǐ tīng, tā chàng de <u>duō(me)</u> hǎotīng!
listen, <u>how</u> lovely her singing is!

她写得真漂亮！
tā xiě de <u>zhēn</u> piàoliàng!
her handwriting is <u>really</u> pretty!

这张照片多(么)丑！
zhè zhāng zhàopiàn <u>duō(me)</u> chǒu!
<u>what an</u> ugly photo!

2 Exclamatives with 啊 a

a) Simple exclamatives can be constructed by placing the particle 啊 a at the beginning or end of a clause, typically to express a sigh or gasp.

这里的空气多(么)新鲜啊！
zhèlǐ de kōngqì duō(me) xīnxiān <u>a</u>!
<u>isn't</u> the air fresh in here!

你的中文说得真流利啊！
nǐde Zhōngwén shuō de zhēn liúlì <u>a</u>!
<u>wow</u>, your spoken Chinese is so fluent!

多糟糕啊!
duō zāogāo a!
how terrible! *(sigh)*

啊!真热!
a! zhēn rè!
ah! it's so hot!

啊!你的裙子真好看!
a! nǐde qúnzi zhēn hǎokàn!
wow! your skirt is really pretty!

b) 啊 a can also occur at the end of a clause to express surprise or to allow the speaker to respond to a question with another question. The softer tone of the utterance is also perceived to be more polite.

你是老师啊?
nǐ shì lǎoshī a?
ah! you're a teacher?

你去不去啊?
nǐ qù bú qù a?
oh! are you going?

你知道不知道啊?
nǐ zhīdào bù zhīdào a?
ah! don't you know?

我怎么知道啊?
wǒ zěnme zhīdào a?
hey! how would I know?

3 Exclamatives with 啦 **la**, 呀 **ya**, 哪 **na** and 哇 **wa**

Sometimes 啦 la, 呀 ya, 哪 na and 哇 wa may be used in place of 啊 a to express surprise. The variant is determined by the vowel or consonant that ends the previous word:

❏ When the character that precedes the exclamative ends with 'a', 'e', 'i', 'o' or 'u' in the pinyin, then 呀 ya may be used.

❏ When the character that precedes the exclamative ends with 'n' or 'ng' in the pinyin then 哪 na may be used.

❏ When the character that precedes the exclamative ends with 'ao' or 'ou' in the pinyin then 哇 wa may be used.

❏ If the character preceding the exclamative is the particle 了 le, then it combines with 啊 a to become 啦 la.

你说什么呀?
nǐ shuō shénme <u>ya</u>?
what are you talking about?

我不知道哇!
wǒ bù zhīdào <u>wa</u>!
I don't know!

这条河多长哪!
zhè tiáo hé duō cháng <u>na</u>!
she has a lot of clothes!

我们明天都去啦!
wǒmen míngtiān dōu qù <u>la</u>!
tomorrow, we'll all go together!

10 VERBS

Chinese verbs have only one form. Unlike in English, they do not inflect to indicate person, number or tense (eg 'I go', 'we went'). There are three main classes of verb:

- ❏ Stative verbs
- ❏ Modal verbs
- ❏ Action verbs

A STATIVE VERBS

Stative verbs are used to describe characteristics, a permanent state or a situation whereby no obvious action takes place. Unlike adjectival stative verbs (which are translated as English adjectives, *see* pages 53-4), Chinese stative verbs may be translated as English verbs. The following are examples of stative verbs:

喜欢	想念	怕
xǐhuān	xiǎng niàn	pà
to like	to miss	to fear
爱	像	懂
ài	xiàng	dǒng
to love	to resemble	to understand

In the same way as adjectives, most stative verbs can be preceded by adverbs of degree (*see* pages 56-7):

我很喜欢这本书
wǒ <u>hěn xǐhuān</u> zhè běn shū
(*lit.* I <u>very like</u> this book)
I like this book very much

他真爱说话
tā <u>zhēn ài</u> shuōhuà
he <u>really loves</u> to talk

1 是 shì (to be)

The verb 是 shì (to be) is a stative verb, but is omitted in Chinese when linking a subject to a predicative adjective, known as an adjectival stative verb (*see* **pages 53–4**). However, 是 shì must be used when linking a subject noun to another *noun* or *pronoun*, for example when talking about someone's profession, identity or nationality. Note that it is not possible to use an adverb of degree with 是 shì:

我是章子怡　　　　　　　他是王力宏
wǒ <u>shì</u> Zhāng Zǐyí　　　　　tā <u>shì</u> Wáng Lìhóng
I <u>am</u> Ziyi Zhang　　　　　　he <u>is</u> Wang Lee Hom

我们是学生　　　　　　　他们是足球员
wǒmen <u>shì</u> xuéshēng　　　　　tāmen <u>shì</u> zúqiúyuán
we <u>are</u> students　　　　　　they <u>are</u> footballers

2 有 yǒu (to have)

The verb 有 yǒu (to have) is a stative verb that can be used to express possession:

我有三只红铅笔
wǒ <u>yǒu</u> sānzhī hóng qiānbǐ
I <u>have</u> three red pencils

It can also be used to express 'there is/are/was/were' in the construction 'location + 有 yǒu + noun':

书包里有两只红笔
shūbāo lǐ <u>yǒu</u> liǎngzhī hóng bǐ
in the school bag <u>there are</u> two red pens

Note that 有 yǒu is *always* negated by 没 méi:

我没有钱　　　　　　　　桌上没有钱
wǒ <u>méiyǒu</u> qián　　　　　　　zhuō shàng <u>méiyǒu</u> qián
I <u>don't have</u> any money　　　<u>there is no</u> money on the table

B MODAL VERBS

Modal verbs precede action verbs. They are used to provide
additional information about the mood of the action verb, for
example to express obligation, permission or need *etc*. The most
common modal verbs are:

应该 yīnggāi	should, ought to
得 děi	to have to
必须 bìxū	to be obliged to
会 huì	to know how to
能 néng	to be able to, to be allowed to
可以 kěyǐ	to be allowed to
要 yào	to want to
想要 xiǎngyào	to wish to, would like to
需要 xūyào	to need to, to be required to
愿意 yuànyì	to be willing to

1 Use of modal verbs

a) Obligation

应该 yīnggāi (should, ought to), 得 děi (to have to) and 必须 bìxū
(to be obliged to) all express degrees of obligation. In order to
understand when each is used, it is helpful to compare them in
their affirmative (positive) forms:

我应该帮你
wǒ yīnggāi bāng nǐ
I <u>should</u> help you

我得帮你
wǒ děi bāng nǐ
I <u>have to</u> help you

我必须帮你
wǒ bìxū bāng nǐ
I <u>am obliged to</u> help you

应该 yīnggāi can also be used with the negator 不 bù to express 'shouldn't, ought not to':

你不应该说谎
nǐ **bù yīnggāi** shuōhuǎng
you **shouldn't** tell lies

However, when expressing the negative form of 得 děi or 必须 bìxū it is necessary to use either 不用 búyòng or 不必 búbì, which both translate roughly as 'don't need to' or 'need not':

我不用考虑了
wǒ **búyòng** kǎolǜ le
I **don't need to** think it over

你不必服从命令
nǐ **búbì** fúcóng mìnglìng
you **need not** obey orders

> ## Note
> 不得 bùdé (not permitted) often occurs in public signs and notices indicating rules or things that are forbidden:
> 不得入内!
> **bùdé** rù nèi!
> **no** entry!

b) Ability and permission

会 huì (to know how to), 能 néng (to be able to, to be allowed to) and 可以 kěyǐ (to be allowed to) all express degrees of ability or permission.

The verb 能 néng is used to express what one is *physically able* to do. In contrast, 会 huì is used to express what one has *learnt* to do, or *knows how* to do. Compare the following sentences:

我能说英语
wǒ **néng** shuō Yīngyǔ
I **can** speak English
(I have the ability to speak English)

我会说英语
wǒ <u>huì</u> shuō Yīngyǔ
I <u>can</u> speak English
(I have learnt to speak English)

> ### Note
>
> The modal verb 会 huì can also be used to express intentions or
> decisions (will):
>
> 我会回来   我明天会去体育馆
> wǒ <u>huì</u> huílái   wǒ míngtiān <u>huì</u> qù tǐyùguǎn
> I <u>will</u> come back   I <u>will</u> go to the gym tomorrow

The verb 能 néng can also be used to indicate what one is
logically permitted to do. In contrast, 可以 kěyǐ is used to express
what one is *allowed* to do, given the permission of another.
Compare the following:

下课了，我们能出去玩
xiàkè le, wǒmen <u>néng</u> chūqù wán
the lesson's over, we <u>can</u> go out to play *(we are able to)*

下课了，我们可以出去玩
xiàkè le, wǒmen <u>kěyǐ</u> chūqù wán
the lesson's over, we <u>can</u> go out to play *(we have permission)*

可以 kěyǐ can be used in a tag question with the question
particle 吗 ma to check that the listener is in agreement or gives
his/her permission:

我们谈谈，可以吗?
wǒmen tántan, <u>kěyǐ</u> ma?
let's talk, <u>OK</u>?

In the negative, 可以 kěyǐ is used to forbid. Compare the
following:

你的喉咙痛，所以不能吃东西
nǐde hóulóng tòng, suǒyǐ <u>bù néng</u> chī dōngxi
you have a sore throat so <u>are not allowed to</u> eat

在图书馆里，不可以吃东西
zài túshūguǎn lǐ, bù kěyǐ chī dōngxi
eating <u>is forbidden</u> in the library

c) Wishes

Both 要 yào (to want to) and 想要 xiǎngyào (to wish to, would like to) are used in requests or to state one's intentions. They can be used interchangeably, although 想要 xiǎngyào is a more polite alternative:

我要去游泳
wǒ <u>yào</u> qù yóuyǒng
I <u>want to</u> go swimming

我想要去游泳
wǒ <u>xiǎngyào</u> qù yóuyǒng
I <u>would like to</u> go swimming

d) Need

需要 xūyào (to need to, to be required to):

你需要跟他说
nǐ <u>xūyào</u> gēn tā shuō
you <u>need to</u> speak to him

e) Willingness

你愿意参加下个星期的挑战吗？
nǐ <u>yuànyì</u> cānjiā xiàge xīngqī de tiǎozhàn ma?
will you be <u>willing to</u> take the challenge next week?

2 Position of modal verbs

a) Modal verbs often occur after 都 dōu (all), 不 bù (not) and 也 yě (too, as well, also) and before an action verb:

他们都应该去
tāmen <u>dōu yīnggāi</u> qù
(*lit.* they <u>all should</u> go)
they should all go

他们不应该去
tāmen <u>bù yīnggāi</u> qù
(*lit.* they <u>not should</u> go)
they shouldn't go

他们也应该去
tāmen yě yīnggāi qù
(*lit.* they <u>too should</u> go)
they should go too

b) Modal verbs are often placed before expressions of time, such as
常常 chángchang (frequently, often) and 已经 yǐjīng (already):

他们应该常常去
tāmen yīnggāi chángchang qù
(*lit.* they <u>should often</u> go)
they should go often

他们应该已经去了
tāmen yīnggāi yǐjīng qù le
(*lit.* they <u>should already</u> have left)
they should have already left

 C ACTION VERBS

Action verbs are primarily used to express activities (eg 走 zǒu 'to
walk', 跑 pǎo 'to run', 站 zhàn 'to stand', 坐 zuò 'to sit'), processes
(eg 换 huàn 'to change', 长 zhǎng 'to grow') and sensations (eg
痛 tòng 'to ache', 疼 téng 'to hurt').

1 Negation

Action verbs are negated with 不 bù in the present or 没 méi in the
past. For example:

我去机场		我不去机场
wǒ qù jīchǎng	→	wǒ bú qù jīchǎng
I'm <u>going</u> to the airport		I'm <u>not going</u> to the airport
他吃早饭		他没吃早饭
tā chī zǎofàn	→	tā méi chī zǎofàn
he <u>eats</u> breakfast		he <u>did not eat</u> breakfast

2 Aspect markers

Action verbs do not change their form to show tense. Instead, the
time when an action takes place can be indicated by an expression
of time, the context or one of the aspect markers 了 le, 过 guò
or 着 zhe. These function in several different ways, but are most
commonly placed after an action verb in order to indicate whether
an action is completed or in progress. Note that aspect markers
cannot be used with stative verbs.

了 le	for completed actions
过 guò	for completed experiences in the past
着 zhe	for actions in progress or developing

For example:

她看了那个电影了
tā kàn-le nàge diànyǐng le
she saw/has seen that movie

她看过那个电影
tā kàn-guò nàge diànyǐng
she had seen that movie before

她看着那个电影
tā kàn-zhe nàge diànyǐng
she is/was watching that movie

a) 了 le

  i) When 了 le is placed directly after the action verb, it indicates
     completion of an action:

我吃了三个汉堡包
wǒ chī-le sān ge hànbǎobāo
I ate three hamburgers

我睡了十五分钟
wǒ shuì-le shí-wǔ fēnzhōng
I slept for fifteen minutes

了 le can be used to indicate completion of an action in any
tense. If it is not obvious from the context when the event
is occurring, then it is necessary to precede the verb with an
expression of time:

Habitual

我每天吃了饭，就看书
wǒ měitiān chī-le fàn, jiù kànshū
every day after I finish my meal, I read a book

In the future

我明天吃了饭，就看书
wǒ míngtiān chī-le fàn, jiù kànshū
after I've finished my meal tomorrow, I will read a book

In the past

我昨天吃了饭，就看书了
wǒ zuótiān chī-le fàn, jiù kànshū le
yesterday, after I had finished my meal, I read a book

ii) To indicate the duration or frequency of a completed action, the
construction 'action verb + 了 le + expression of time' is used:

他等了一天
tā děng-le yì tiān
he waited for a day

这本书，我看了两次
zhè běn shū, wǒ kàn-le liǎngcì
I had read this book twice

她写了三个钟头
tā xiě-le sānge zhōngtou
she wrote for three hours

他们讨论了很多次
tāmen tǎolùn-le hěnduō cì
they have discussed this many times

> Note
>
> To indicate the precise time at which an action occurs or occurred, the expression of time is placed *before* the verb and no aspect marker is required. Compare the following examples:
>
> 我在中国住了两年
> wǒ zài Zhōngguó zhù-le liǎng nián
> I <u>lived</u> in China <u>for two years</u>
>
> 我两年前住在中国
> wǒ liǎng nián qián zhù zài Zhōngguó
> <u>two years ago</u>, I <u>lived</u> in China

iii) 了 le can also be used at the end of a sentence with 已经 yǐjīng (already) to indicate that an action has been sustained up to the point of one's speech. Compare the following:

我学了三年中文
wǒ xué-le sān nián Zhōngwén
I <u>studied</u> Chinese for three years (*a completed action*)

我已经学了三年中文了
wǒ yǐjīng xué-le sān nián Zhōngwén le
I <u>have already studied</u> Chinese for three years (*up to this point*)

iv) 快 kuài, 要 yào and 快要 kuàiyào (to be about to, to be going to, to be soon to) can all be used interchangeably with an action verb + 了 le to indicate an imminent action. Note that this construction conveys a sense of urgency:

快下雨了!
kuài xiàyǔ le!
it's <u>going to</u> rain!

要上课了!
yào shàngkè le!
the class <u>is about to</u> begin!

v) 了 le can be used at the end of a sentence to indicate a change of situation or a new state:

他死了
tā sǐ le
he's dead

我懂法语了
wǒ dǒng Fǎyǔ le
I now understand French

> ## Note
>
> 了 le can also be used at the end of a statement to indicate excess:
>
> | 太贵了! | 太多了! | 好极了 |
> |---|---|---|
> | tài guì <u>le</u>! | tài duō <u>le</u>! | hǎo jí <u>le</u> |
> | <u>too</u> expensive! | <u>too</u> much! | it's <u>extremely</u> good |

b) 过 guò

   i) When the aspect marker 过 guò is placed directly after an action verb, it can be used to describe an experience in the indefinite past:

他去过中国	我吃过春卷
tā <u>qù-guò</u> Zhōngguó	wǒ <u>chī-guò</u> chūnjuǎn
he <u>has been</u> to China	I <u>have had</u> spring rolls before

   ii) The negator 没 méi is placed before an action verb with 过 guò to describe a negative experience in the indefinite past:

他没去过中国	我没吃过春卷
tā <u>méi</u> qù-guò Zhōngguó	wǒ <u>méi</u> chī-guò chūnjuǎn
he <u>has not been</u> to China	I <u>haven't eaten</u> spring rolls before

> ## Note
>
> The distinction between a completed experience, expressed with 过 guò, and a completed action, expressed with 了 le, is subtle. Compare the following:
>
> 他当过老师
> tā <u>dāng-guò</u> lǎoshī
> he <u>had been/was</u> a teacher (but is no longer)
>
> 他当了老师
> tā <u>dāng-le</u> lǎoshī
> he <u>became</u> a teacher (and still is)

c) 着 zhe

　　i) When 着 zhe is placed directly after an action verb, it can be used to indicate that an action is ongoing:

同学们笑着
tóngxuémén xiào-zhe
students <u>are laughing</u>

她穿着红鞋子
tā <u>chuān-zhe</u> hóng xiézi
she <u>is wearing</u> red shoes

　　ii) The construction 'verb + 着 zhe + verb' is used to indicate that one action is taking place at the same time as another.

他忙着准备考试
tā <u>máng-zhe</u> zhǔnbèi kǎoshì
he <u>is busy preparing</u> for the exam

他笑着说。。。
tā <u>xiào-zhe</u> shuō ...
he <u>smiled</u> and <u>said</u> ...

　　iii) 着 zhe can also be used with 正在 zhèngzài, 正 zhèng or 在 zài, which all precede the verb, to emphasize the fact that an action is in progress:

他正说着!
tā <u>zhèng shuō-zhe</u>!
he <u>is talking</u>!

他在说着!
tā <u>zài shuō-zhe</u>!
he <u>is talking</u>!

3 把 bǎ

In Chinese, the preposition 把 bǎ is used to mark the direct object and to indicate that its form, state or location has changed in some way. In other words, it emphasizes the *result* of an action verb. 把 bǎ appears between the subject and the direct object of the verb and therefore changes the word order of the sentence to 'subject-object-verb'. Note that the object that follows 把 bǎ is always a *definite* noun (see **page 42**).

a) 把 bǎ + object + verb + 了 le

In this type of construction, 了 le indicates that the action is complete and 把 bǎ indicates that the object has changed in some way as a result of that action. For example:

他把书拿来了
tā bǎ shū nálái le
he <u>has brought</u> the book <u>here</u>

> ## Note
>
> In an imperative sentence with 把 bǎ (*see* page 67), 了 le occurs at the end of the statement, not to indicate a completed action but to show that the listener is *required* to complete the action:
>
> 把饭吃了!
> bǎ fàn chī-le!
> <u>finish</u> eating the meal!

b) 把 bǎ + object + verb + 着 zhe

把 bǎ is used with 着 zhe to convey the ongoing change of state or location of an object:

把书开着	他把书带着
bǎ shū kāi-zhe	tā bǎ shū dài-zhe
<u>leaving</u> the book <u>open</u>	he <u>is carrying</u> the book

c) Using 把 bǎ with a directional complement

For more on directional complements, see pages 92-3.
When referring to the movement of an action, directional complements such as 来 lái (come), 去 qù (go) and 上去 shàngqù (go up) may be placed after a verb.
The '把 bǎ + object + verb + directional complement' construction can be used to express 'take something to somewhere':

她把车开进来了	把苹果带回去
tā bǎ chē kāi jìnlái le	bǎ píngguǒ dài huíqù
she <u>has</u> driven the car <u>in</u>	take the apple <u>back</u>

d) Using 把 bǎ with a complement of result

For more on complements of result, see **pages 89–92.**

When indicating the specific outcome of an action, 把 bǎ can be used with a complement of result such as 完 wán (to finish) or 错 cuò (to be wrong) in the construction '把 bǎ + object + verb + complement of result':

他把饭吃完了
tā bǎ fàn chī-<u>wán</u> le
he has <u>finished</u> eating all the meal

他把名字写错了
tā bǎ míngzi xiě-<u>cuò</u> le
he wrote the name <u>wrong</u>

e) Using 把 bǎ with a frequency complement

把 bǎ can occur in the construction '把 bǎ + object + verb + frequency complement':

把衣服洗两次	他把书看了三遍了
bǎ yīfu xǐ <u>liǎngcì</u>	tā bǎ shū kàn-le <u>sān biàn</u> le
to wash the clothes <u>twice</u>	he had read the book <u>three times</u>

f) 把 bǎ with a modal verb or negator

When 把 bǎ is used with a modal verb or in the negative, it appears *after* the modal verb or the negator. Note that 把 bǎ sentences are negated with 没 méi or 别 bié:

他应该把书放在桌上
tā <u>yīnggāi bǎ</u> shū fàng zài zhuō shàng
he <u>should</u> have put the book on the table

他没把书放在桌上
tā <u>méi bǎ</u> shū fàng zài zhuō shàng
he <u>didn't</u> put the book on the table

g) 把 bǎ is not used with the following verbs:

相信	喜欢	希望	是
xiāngxìn	xǐhuān	xīwàng	shì
to believe in	to like; to prefer	to hope	to be

有 yǒu to have	像 xiàng to seem	碰见 pèngjiàn to meet	懂 dǒng to understand
遇到 yùdào to come across	认识 rènshì to recognize	看见 kànjiàn to see	听见 tīngjiàn to hear
出发 chūfā to start, set off	觉得 juéde to feel; to be aware		

Note

In a sentence with 把 bǎ, the verb can be repeated to indicate the casualness of an action or to soften the tone of a demand. For example:

把报纸看看
bǎ bàozhǐ kàn-kan
to have a quick look at the newspaper

11 COMPLEMENTS

Complements are words or phrases required to complete the meaning of certain words in Chinese. They most typically come after a verb or an adjective and can be broadly divided into the following categories.

A COMPLEMENTS OF DEGREE

These are elements used to provide additional information about the main verb of a sentence; specifically they provide an assessment of *how* an action is habitually carried out or describe the effect or result of an action.

The structure of a sentence with a complement of degree is 'verb + 得 de + complement'. The complement can be an adjective or verb and can also be preceded and modified by an adverb, such as 很 hěn (very) or 非常 fēicháng (very):

这些男孩吃得很慢
zhèxiē nánhái chī-de hěn màn
these boys eat <u>very slowly</u>

他说得非常流利
tā shuō-de fēicháng liúlì
he speaks <u>very fluently</u>

When the verb takes an object, the verb must be repeated in the construction 'verb + object + verb + 得 de + complement'. Note that the second verb is the main verb and therefore followed by the complement.

你写汉字写得很快
nǐ xiě hànzì xiě-de hěn kuài
you write Chinese characters <u>very fast</u>

他说话说得非常慢
tā shuō huà shuō-de fēicháng màn
(*lit.* he speaks language <u>very slowly</u>)
he speaks <u>very slowly</u>

To form the negative, 不 bù is placed between 得 de and the complement:

他吃得不多
tā chī-de <u>bù</u> duō
he doesn<u>'t</u> eat much

我走得不快
wǒ zǒu-de <u>bú</u> kuài
I don<u>'t</u> walk fast

Complements of degree can also occur with intensifiers such as 得很 dehěn (very) or 极了 jíle (extremely), which appear *after* the complement:

这个男孩吃得快得很
zhège nánhái chī-de kuài <u>dehěn</u>
this boy eats <u>very</u> fast

他唱得高兴极了
tā chàng-de gāoxìng <u>jíle</u>
he is <u>extremely</u> happy singing

 ## B COMPLEMENTS OF RESULT

Complements of result are verbs used to indicate the result of an action. They are typically placed after an action verb. Different complements of result can indicate different qualities or types of result.

In the examples below, compare how the meaning of the action verb (on the left) changes when it is followed by a complement of result (on the right):

听 tīng (to listen)

我喜欢听音乐
wǒ xǐhuān <u>tīng</u> yīnyuè
I like <u>listening</u> to music

听见 tīngjiàn (to hear)

我听见我妈妈在叫我的名字
wǒ <u>tīngjiàn</u> wǒ māma zài jiào
wǒde míngzi
I <u>heard</u> my mother calling my name

看 kàn (to look)

看! 这些玫瑰真漂亮
<u>kàn</u>! zhèxiē méiguì zhēn
   piàoliàng
<u>look</u>! these roses are very pretty

买 mǎi (to buy)

你要买周杰伦最新的专辑吗?
nǐ yào <u>mǎi</u> Zhōu Jiélún zuì xīn de
   zhuānjí ma?
do you want to <u>buy</u> Jay Chou's
   latest album?

看到 kàndào (to see)

在花园里,我看到一些美丽的玫瑰
zài huāyuán lǐ, wǒ <u>kàndào</u> yìxiē
   měilìde méiguì
I <u>saw</u> some pretty roses in the
   garden

买到 mǎidào (to buy)

我买到了周杰伦最新的专辑
wǒ <u>mǎidào</u>-le Zhōu Jiélún zuì xīn
   de zhuānjí
I <u>have bought</u> Jay Chou's latest
   album

1 Common complements of result

a) 见 jiàn indicates perception:

我听见小鸟的歌声
wǒ <u>tīngjiàn</u> xiǎoniǎo de gēshēng
I <u>hear</u> the bird singing

我看见树上的鸟
wǒ <u>kànjiàn</u> shù shàng de niǎo
I <u>see</u> the birds up in the tree

b) 完 wán indicates completion:

我读完了
wǒ <u>dúwán</u> le
I've <u>finished reading</u>

c) 懂 dǒng indicates comprehension:

我听懂你的解释
wǒ <u>tīngdǒng</u> nǐde jiěshì
I <u>understand</u> your explanation

d) 会 huì indicates mastery of a skill:

我学会插花
wǒ <u>xuéhuì</u> chāhuā
I <u>have learnt how to</u> arrange flowers

e) 住 zhù indicates retention:

我会记住你美丽的微笑
wǒ huì jìzhù nǐ měilìde wēixiào
I will <u>remember</u> your beautiful smile

f) 到 dào indicates an expected result:

我接到你的信了
wǒ jiēdào nǐde xìn le
I <u>have received</u> your letter

2 Adjectival stative verbs as complements of result

See also pages 53-4.

Complements of result may also be formed with adjectival stative verbs such as 好 hǎo (good), 对 duì (correct), 错 cuò (wrong) and 清楚 qīngchǔ (clear).

a) 好 hǎo indicates completion:

我准备好了
wǒ zhǔnbèihǎo le
I am <u>finished preparing</u>

b) 对 duì indicates correctness:

你写对了   他猜对了
nǐ xiěduì le   tā cāiduì le
you <u>wrote (it) correctly</u>   he <u>has guessed correctly</u>

c) 错 cuò indicates incorrectness:

他回答错了   你数错了
tā huídácuò le   nǐ shǔcuò le
he <u>answered incorrectly</u>   you <u>counted wrong</u>

d) 清楚 qīngchǔ indicates clarity:

我听清楚了
wǒ tīngqīngchǔ le
I <u>heard clearly</u>

3 Negative complements of result

没 méi (didn't) is often placed *before* the main verb + complement of result to form a negative sentence in the past tense:

我没听懂
wǒ <u>méi</u> tīngdǒng
I <u>didn't</u> understand what I heard

我没看完
wǒ <u>méi</u> kànwán
I <u>didn't</u> finish reading

 C DIRECTIONAL COMPLEMENTS

Verbs that indicate movement often take directional complements, such as 上 shàng (up), 下 xià (down), 进 jìn (in), 出 chū (out), 回 huí (back) and 过 guò (over), to add information about the direction of the action. For example:

跳进池塘
tiàojìn chítáng
jump <u>into</u> the pool

走出厕所
zǒuchū cèsuǒ
walk <u>out of</u> the toilet

跑回教室
pǎohuí jiàoshì
run <u>back</u> to the classroom

爬过高山
páguò gāoshān
climb <u>over</u> the mountains

1 来 lái and 去 qù

In the same way as the directional complements listed above, 来 lái (towards) and 去 qù (away from) are frequently used with a verb of movement to indicate whether the action is moving towards or away from the speaker:

请把铅笔拿来
qǐng bǎ qiānbǐ nálái
please <u>bring</u> the pencil <u>here</u>

请把铅笔拿去
qǐng bǎ qiānbǐ náqù
please <u>take</u> the pencil <u>away</u>

2 Compound directional complements

来 lái and 去 qù can form compound directional complements with 上 shàng (up), 下 xià (down), 进 jìn (in), 出 chū (out), 回 huí (back) and 过 guò (over) to specify the direction of the action *and* its relation to the speaker. For example:

请开进来
qǐng kāi jìnlái
please drive in
(towards the speaker)

你先走进去
nǐ xiān zǒu jìnqù
you walk in first
(away from the speaker)

拿出来!
ná chūlái!
bring (it) out!
(towards the speaker)

不要跑出去
búyào pǎo chūqù
don't run out
(away from the speaker)

我们要爬上去
wǒmen yào pá shàngqù
we'd like to climb up
(away from the speaker)

请看过来!
qǐng kàn guòlái!
please look over here
(towards the speaker)

If a compound directional complement is followed by a location noun then 来 lái and 去 qù must occur *after* it. Compare these two sentences:

他已经回去了
tā yǐjīng huíqù le
he has already gone (away)

他已经回家去了
tā yǐjīng huí jiā qù le
he has already gone home

 ## D POTENTIAL COMPLEMENTS

Potential complements are formed with complements of result or direction and can therefore express the ability or inability to achieve an action or move something in a certain direction.

Although they are similar to 'be able to', 'can' and 'can't' in English, potential complements differ from the modal verbs that express ability (会 huì, 能 néng and 可以 kěyǐ) in that they indicate a result that the speaker believes to be possible or impossible.

1 Positive potential complements

Positive potential complements can be formed by placing the
particle 得 de between a verb and a complement of result or a
directional complement, for example:

> 我看得到他
> wǒ <u>kàndedào</u> ta
> I <u>can see</u> him

> 这个山不太高，我爬得上
> zhège shān bú tài gāo, wǒ <u>pádeshàng</u>
> I <u>can climb up</u> this mountain, it is not too high

2 Negative potential complements

Negative potential complements indicate inability and can be
formed by placing the negator 不 bù between a verb and a
complement of result or a directional complement, for example:

> 我看不到他
> wǒ <u>kànbúdào</u> tā
> I <u>cannot see</u> him

> 车库门太小，我的车开不进
> chēkù mén tài xiǎo, wǒde chē <u>kāibújìn</u>
> I <u>can't drive into</u> the garage, the door is too small

12 PREPOSITIONS

In Chinese, prepositions are commonly referred to as 'coverbs' because they are almost always used with a verb.

A POSITION OF PREPOSITIONS

1 Preposition + verb

Unlike in English, Chinese prepositions appear before the verb. For example the preposition 给 gěi meaning 'for' or 'to':

我给他买了生日礼物了
wǒ gěi tā mǎi-le shēngrì lǐwù le
I've bought a birthday present for him

2 Negator + preposition

Negators, such as 没 méi or 不 bù appear directly before the preposition, rather than before the verb:

我没给他买生日礼物
wǒ méi gěi tā mǎi shēngrì lǐwù
I didn't buy a birthday gift for him

3 Adverb + preposition

When used with an adverb, the preposition occurs after the adverb:

我已经给他买了生日礼物了
wǒ yǐjīng gěi tā mǎi-le shēngrì lǐwù le
I already bought a birthday present for him

他总是给我买礼物
tā zǒngshì gěi wǒ mǎi lǐwù
he is always buying gifts for me

4 Modal verb + preposition

Modal verbs occur before prepositions:

你应该给他打电话
nǐ yīnggāi gěi tā dǎ diànhuà
(*lit.* you <u>should</u> <u>to</u> him call)
you <u>should</u> give him a call

For more on modal verbs, see pages 75-9.

 B PREPOSITIONS OF TIME AND LOCATION

1 在 zài (at, in, on) + time or location + verb

她在英格兰学习
tā zài Yīnggélán xuéxí
she <u>is</u> studying <u>in</u> England

爸爸在家工作
Bàba zài jiā gōngzuò
Father <u>is</u> working <u>at</u> home

Note that 在 zài can be omitted in spoken Chinese when used to express time, but not location:

(在)夏天，我们常常来这里散步
(zài) xiàtiān, wǒmen chángcháng lái zhèlǐ sànbù
<u>in</u> summer, we often come here for walks

When a more formal tone is required, 于 yú (at, in, on) can be used in place of 在 zài, for example:

她目前于英格兰学习
tā mùqián yú Yīnggélán xuéxí
<u>at</u> present, she <u>is</u> studying <u>in</u> England

2 从 cóng (since/from)

a) 从 cóng can be used before an expression of time to mean 'since' or 'from':

从昨天
cóng zuótiān
<u>since</u> yesterday

从现在
cóng xiànzài
<u>from</u> now

从 cóng can also occur with an expression of time + 开始 kāishǐ or 起 qǐ to express 'starting from...':

从现在开始

<u>cóng</u> xiànzài <u>kāishǐ</u>

<u>starting from</u> now

他从八月开始学中文

tā <u>cóng</u> bāyuè <u>kāishǐ</u> xué Zhōngwén

(*lit.* he <u>beginning from</u> August starts learning Chinese)

he starts learning Chinese from August

从明天起，我要天天跑步

<u>cóng</u> míngtiān <u>qǐ</u>, wǒ yào tiāntiān pǎobù

<u>starting from</u> tomorrow, I want to go jogging everyday

从 cóng often occurs with 到 dào (to) to mean 'from ... to ...':

从七月到九月是学校假期

<u>cóng</u> qīyuè <u>dào</u> jiǔyuè shì xuéxiào jiàqī

school holidays are <u>from</u> July <u>to</u> September

b) 从 cóng can be used with an expression of location + a verb of movement, such as 来 lái (to come from), 去 qù (to go from) or 出发 chūfā (to set off, to set out):

他从上海来

tā <u>cóng</u> Shànghǎi <u>lái</u>

he <u>comes from</u> Shanghai

他明天从上海去

tā míngtiān <u>cóng</u> Shànghǎi <u>qù</u>

he <u>leaves from</u> Shanghai tomorrow

他明天从上海出发

tā míngtiān <u>cóng</u> Shànghǎi <u>chūfā</u>

he <u>sets out from</u> Shanghai tomorrow

c) 从 cóng may also be used with 到 dào (to) to express distance between two locations:

从我家到学校不远

<u>cóng</u> wǒ jiā <u>dào</u> xuéxiào bù yuǎn

(*lit.* <u>from</u> my house <u>to</u> school not far)

my house is not far from school

3 到 dào (to)

a) 到 dào often occurs with an expression of location + 去 qù (to go) or another verb:

我明天到上海去
wǒ míngtiān dào Shànghǎi qù
tomorrow I go to Shanghai

他到医院看病
tā dào yīyuàn kànbìng
he went to the hospital to see the doctor

b) 到 dào can be used with an expression of time to mean 'up to' or 'not until':

他到昨天才看完那本书
tā dào zuótiān cái kànwán nàběn shū
it took him up to yesterday to finish reading the book

他要到明天才会来
tā yào dào míngtiān cái huì lái
he is not arriving until tomorrow

4 往 wǎng and 向 xiàng (towards, in the direction of)

Both 往 wǎng and 向 xiàng can be used before an expression of location to mean 'towards':

这班火车是往北京去的
zhèbān huǒchē shì wǎng Běijīng qù de
this train is headed for Beijing

他向火车站走了
tā xiàng huǒchē zhàn zǒu le
he walked towards the train station

5 离 lí (distance from)

The construction 'location + 离 lí + location + distance' can be used to express a distance between two places:

> 我家离体育馆两公里
> wǒ jiā lí tǐyùguǎn liǎng gōnglǐ
> (*lit.* my house <u>from</u> gymnasium 2 km)
> the gymnasium is 2 km from my house

> 我家离体育馆很近
> wǒ jiā lí tǐyùguǎn hěn jìn
> (*lit.* my house <u>from</u> gymnasium very close)
> my house is very close to the gymnasium

Note that 'distance from' can also be conveyed using 从 cóng and 到 dào. *See* 2 c).

C SOME PARTICULAR CASES

1 对 duì

a) 对 duì is generally used before a noun to express 'towards':

> 老师对我们很友善
> lǎoshī <u>duì</u> wǒmen hěn yǒushàn
> the teacher is very friendly <u>towards</u> us

b) 对 duì is often used with 说 shuō (to say, to tell):

> 他对我说，他明天要去中国
> tā <u>duì</u> wǒ <u>shuō</u>, tā míngtiān yào qù Zhōngguó
> he told me he is leaving for China tomorrow

c) 对 duì can be expressed as 'at':

> 他没说什么，只对我笑
> tā méi shuō shénme, zhǐ <u>duì</u> wǒ xiào
> he didn't say anything, just smiled <u>at</u> me

他对黑板发呆
tā <u>duì</u> hēibǎn fādāi
he stared blankly <u>at</u> the blackboard

d) 对 duì can be used to express feelings or attitudes 'about' or 'towards' something or someone:

他对学习很认真
tā <u>duì</u> xuéxí hěn rènzhēn
he is very conscientious <u>about</u> his studies

2 跟 gēn

a) The '跟 gēn + person' construction can be used to express 'with':

昨天他跟我打了网球
zuótiān tā <u>gēn</u> wǒ dǎ-le wǎngqiú
yesterday, he played tennis <u>with</u> me

In this instance, 跟 gēn could be replaced by 同 tóng or 和 hé to express 'with':

昨天他同我打了网球
zuótiān tā <u>tóng</u> wǒ dǎ-le wǎngqiú
yesterday, he played tennis <u>with</u> me

昨天他和我打了网球
zuótiān tā <u>hé</u> wǒ dǎ-le wǎngqiú
yesterday, he played tennis <u>with</u> me

b) 跟 gēn can occur with 一样 yíyàng to express 'the same as' or 'as ... as':

他的书包跟我的一样
tāde shūbāo <u>gēn</u> wǒde <u>yíyàng</u>
his school bag is <u>the same as</u> mine

他的书包跟我的一样便宜
tāde shūbāo <u>gēn</u> wǒde <u>yíyàng</u> piányi
his school bag is <u>as cheap as</u> mine

3 给 gěi

a) 给 gěi can be used before an indirect object when referring to making a phone call, writing to somebody or similar actions:

我每个星期给妈妈写信

wǒ měige xīngqī gěi māma xiěxìn

every week, I write a letter to my mother

Unlike in English, where the preposition 'to' is not always expressed (eg 'I wrote my mother a letter'), in Chinese 给 gěi must be included. For example:

他昨天给我打了一个电话

tā zuótiān gěi wǒ dǎ-le yíge diànhuà

yesterday, he gave me a call

b) 给 gěi may be used to express 'for' when performing an action for someone else:

我给他买了一本小说　　　　　我给爸爸洗车

wǒ gěi tā mǎi-le yìběn xiǎoshuō　　　wǒ gěi Bàba xǐchē

I bought a novel for him　　　　　I washed the car for Dad

c) When 给 gěi can be translated as 'to' it is generally placed directly after the verb:

我送他一本英文小说　　　　　我还给他钱了

wǒ sòng-gěi tā yìběn yīngwén xiǎoshuō　　wǒ huán-gěi tā qián le

I gave an English novel to him　　　I returned the money to him

我卖他我的电脑了　　　　　　我借给她我的自行车了

wǒ mài-gěi tā wǒde diànnǎo le　　　wǒ jie-gěi tā wǒde zìxíngchē le

I sold my computer to him　　　　I lent my bike to her

4 为 wèi

为 wèi suggests doing or feeling something 'for the sake of' someone or something:

我为生活而写作　　　　　　　父母为我们辛苦工作

wǒ wèi shēnghuó ér xiězuò　　　fùmǔ wèi wǒmen xīnkǔ gōngzuò

I write for a living　　　　　　our parents worked hard for us

他考试不及格，我们很为他难过

tā kǎoshì bù jígé, wǒmen hěn <u>wèi</u> tā nánguò

he failed his exams, we feel sorry <u>for</u> him

5 替 tì

替 tì may be used to express 'for' or 'on behalf of' someone:

我不会说法文，请你替我说

wǒ búhuì shuō Fǎwén, qǐng nǐ <u>tì</u> wǒ shuō

I can't speak French, please speak <u>for me</u>

我今天不舒服，请你替我请假

wǒ jīntiān bù shūfu, qǐng nǐ <u>tì</u> wǒ qǐngjià

I'm not feeling well; please ask for sick leave <u>on my behalf</u>

6 由 yóu

a) 由 yóu can be used to express 'by' or 'up to' and conveys a sense of responsibility:

这个工作由他完成

zhège gōngzuò <u>yóu</u> tā wánchéng

this piece of work was completed <u>by</u> him

这件事由她跟老师说

zhèjiàn shì <u>yóu</u> tā gēn lǎoshī shuō

it's <u>up to</u> her to speak to the teacher about this matter

b) For a more formal tone, 由 yóu can replace 从 cóng when used with an expression of time or location:

他们由上海国际机场起飞

tāmen <u>yóu Shànghǎi</u> guójì jīchǎng qǐfēi

they take off <u>from Shanghai</u> International airport

学校暑假由七月开始

xuéxiào shǔjià <u>yóu qīyuè</u> kāishǐ

school holidays begin <u>from July</u>

It can also be used with 到 dào to specify a period between two expressions of time:

每天由上午十点到十点半休息

měitiān <u>yóu</u> shàngwǔ shí diǎn <u>dào</u> shí diǎn bàn xiūxi

break time is <u>from</u> 10 <u>to</u> 10.30 am everyday

c) 由 yóu can be used to refer to the components of an item:

这个队是由八个国家组成的

zhège duì shì <u>yóu</u> bāge guójiā zǔchéng de

this team consists <u>of</u> 8 countries

这本集子是由诗、散文和短篇小说三部分组成的

zhèběn jízi shì <u>yóu</u> shī, sǎnwén hé duǎnpiān xiǎoshuō sān bùfèn zǔchéng de

this collection is made up <u>of</u> three parts: poems, essays and short stories

D DISYLLABIC PREPOSITIONS

Although most prepositions in Chinese are words of one syllable, some pairs and groups of words can operate together like a single preposition, and normally occur at the beginning of sentences.

1 为了 wèile (in order to, for the sake of)

为了上班方便，她全家搬到市中心

wèile shàngbān fāngbiàn, tā quán jiā bān dào shìzhōngxīn

<u>for</u> the convenience of getting to work, her whole family moved to the city centre

为了健康，他一星期运动三次

wèile jiànkāng, tā yì xīngqī yùndòng sān cì

<u>in order to</u> stay healthy, he exercises three times a week

2 对于 duìyú (as to, about)

对于他说的话，你别相信

<u>duìyú</u> tā shuō de huà, nǐ bié xiāngxìn

<u>as to</u> what he said, you shouldn't believe him

3 关于 guānyú (with regard to, regarding)

关于这件事，我建议我们再仔细考虑
guānyú zhèjiàn shì, wǒ jiànyì wǒmen zài zǐxì kǎolǜ
<u>regarding</u> this matter, I suggest we consider it carefully

4 至于 zhìyú (as for)

至于技术，我们应当努力赶上世界最高水平
zhìyú jìshù, wǒmen yīngdāng nǔlì gǎnshàng shìjiè zuìgāo shuǐpíng
<u>as for</u> technology, we should do our best to reach the world's
　　highest level

5 按照 ànzhào (in accordance with, according to)

按照惯例
ànzhào guànlì
<u>according to</u> the customary practice

按照学校的规定，学生一定要穿校服
ànzhào xuéxiàode guīdìng, xuéshēng yídìng yào chuān xiàofú
<u>in accordance with</u> school regulations, students must wear uniform

6 根据 gēnjù (based on, on the basis of)

根据他的看法，学生一年学五百个汉字没有问题
gēnjù tāde kànfǎ, xuéshēng yì nián xué wǔ bǎi ge hànzì méiyǒu wèntí
<u>based on</u> his opinion, it's possible for a student to learn 500 Chinese
　　characters in a year

7 除了 chúle (+ 以外 yǐwài) (except, besides)

除了星期日，我每天都上班
chúle xīngqīrì, wǒ měitiān dōu shàngbān
I work every day <u>except</u> Sunday

除了你以外，大家都去
chúle nǐ yǐwài, dàjiā dōu qù
we are all going, <u>except</u> you

除了化学以外，我们还喜欢学习物理
<u>chúle</u> huàxué <u>yǐwài</u>, wǒmen hái xǐhuān xuéxí wùlǐ
<u>besides</u> chemistry we like to study physics

 E PASSIVE VOICE

The passive voice is used to talk about an action *being done* (by someone or something). It is much less common in Chinese than in English, as it is often associated with bad news or misfortune. The prepositions 被 bèi, 叫 jiào, 让 ràng and 给 gěi (all meaning 'by') can be used interchangeably in the construction 'object + preposition + agent + verb' to express an action in the passive voice. The agent is the person or thing performing the action.

我的钱被他偷了
wǒde qián <u>bèi</u> tā tōu le
my money was stolen <u>by</u> him

帽子被风刮掉了
màozi <u>bèi</u> fēng guādiào le
the hat was blown off

盘子叫她拿走了
pánzi <u>jiào</u> tā názǒu le
the plate was taken away <u>by</u> her

太阳让云彩遮住了
tàiyáng <u>ràng</u> yúncǎi zhēzhù le
the sun was hidden <u>by</u> clouds

她的衣服叫汗水湿透了
tāde yīfú <u>jiào</u> hànshuǐ shītòu le
her clothes were soaked <u>with</u> sweat

我要的书让同学拿走了
wǒ yàode shū <u>ràng</u> tóngxué názǒu le
the book I wanted was taken away <u>by</u> a classmate

他的自行车给雨淋湿了
tāde zìxíngchē <u>gěi</u> yǔ línshī le
his bicycle was soaked <u>by</u> the rain

报纸给风吹走了
bàozhǐ <u>gěi</u> fēng chuīzǒu le
the newspaper was blown away <u>by</u> the wind

13 CONJUNCTIONS

Conjunctions are used to link and express relationships between words and clauses. Conjunctions in Chinese can be split into four main categories:

❏ Coordinating conjunctions
❏ Correlative conjunctions
❏ Cohesive conjunctions
❏ Subordinating conjunctions

A COORDINATING CONJUNCTIONS

In Chinese, coordinating conjunctions can only be used to link two similar words or groups of words (eg nouns with nouns or verb phrases with verb phrases). The following are the main coordinating conjunctions in Chinese:

1 Linking nouns and noun phrases

和 hé	
跟 gēn	
同 tóng	and
与 yǔ	
还有 háiyǒu	also, too

a) 和 **hé**, 跟 **gēn**, 同 **tóng** and 与 **yǔ** (and)

水果和蔬菜都很新鲜
shuǐguǒ <u>hé</u> shūcài dōu hěn xīnxiān
all fruit <u>and</u> vegetables are fresh

他跟我是同学
tā gēn wǒ shì tóngxué
he _and_ I are schoolmates

我同你在一起
wǒ tóng nǐ zài yìqǐ
you _and_ I are together

环境污染与工业有密切的关系
huánjìng wūrǎn yǔ gōngyè yǒu mìqiède guānxì
environmental pollution _and_ industrialisation are closely related

These conjunctions can be used interchangeably, but note that
同 tóng and 与 yǔ are generally used in a more formal context.

b) 还有 háiyǒu (also, too)

Note that unlike in English, where 'too' occurs at the end of the
sentence, 还有 háiyǒu is inserted between the two nouns or noun
phrases:

我喜欢打篮球, 还有网球
wǒ xǐhuān dǎ lánqiú, háiyǒu wǎngqiú
(_lit._ I like to play basketball _too_ tennis)
I like to play basketball and tennis too

2 Linking verbs and verb phrases

也 yě	and, as well as
还 hái	as well as; still
另外 lìngwài	in addition to, besides
而 ér	and; but; yet

a) 也 yě (and, as well as)

他会说中文, 也会说日语
tā huì shuō Zhōngwén, yě huì shuō Rìyǔ
(_lit._ he speaks Chinese _and_ speaks Japanese)
he speaks Chinese and Japanese

b) 还 hái (as well as; still)

他去了中国，还去了日本
tā qù-le Zhōngguó, hái qù-le Rìběn
(*lit.* he visited China <u>as well as</u> visited Japan)
<u>as well as</u> China, he visited Japan

他来了一年了，还想再多住两年
tā lái-le yì nián le, hái xiǎng zài duō zhù liǎng nián
he's already been here a year, and <u>still</u> wants to stay for another two

c) 另外 lìngwài (in addition to, besides)

我买了一双鞋，另外还买了一双袜子
wǒ mǎi-le yìshuāng xié, lìngwài hái mǎi-le yìshuāng wàzi
<u>besides</u> the pair of shoes, I bought a pair of socks

昨天他看了电影，另外也逛了街
zuótiān tā kàn-le diànyǐng, lìngwài yě guàng-le jiē
<u>in addition to</u> watching a movie yesterday, he went shopping

Note that 另外 lìngwài is often used together with 还 hái and 也 yě.

d) Functions of 而 ér

The conjunction 而 ér is often used in the written form and in formal spoken contexts. It has the meaning 'and' if the two verb phrases it joins are complementary or 'but' if the two phrases are contrasting.

   i) 而 ér (and)

美丽而动人
měilì ér dòngrén
(*lit.* is beautiful <u>and</u> is moving)
it's beautiful and moving

有百利而无一害
yǒu bǎilì ér wú yíhài
gain everything <u>and</u> lose nothing

ii) 而 (but, yet)

> 这领带的颜色艳而不俗
> zhè lǐngdàide yánsè yàn ér bù sú
> this tie is bright <u>but</u> not garish

 B CORRELATIVE CONJUNCTIONS

Correlative conjunctions always appear in pairs and are used to link words or phrases of the same type. The most common correlative conjunctions are:

又 yòu ... 又 yòu	both ... and
也 yě ... 也 yě	both ... and
不但 búdàn ... 而且 érqiě	not only ... but also
一边 yìbiān ... 一边 yìbiān	while, as, at the same time

1 又 yòu ... 又 yòu (both ... and)

This construction is used to link verbs, including adjectival stative verbs:

> 蛋炒饭又好吃又便宜
> dàn chǎofàn yòu hǎochī yòu piányi
> egg fried rice is <u>both</u> delicious <u>and</u> cheap

> 这只猪长得又肥又壮
> zhèzhī zhū zhǎngde yòu féi yòu zhuàng
> this pig has grown <u>both</u> fat <u>and</u> strong

2 也 yě ... 也 yě (both ... and)

This construction is generally used to link verbs only:

> 他也会说中文，也会说日文
> tā yě huì shuō Zhōngwén, yě huì shuō Rìwén
> he can speak <u>both</u> Chinese <u>and</u> Japanese

3 不但 **búdàn ...** 而且 **érqiě** (not only ... but also)

这个酒店不但方便，而且便宜
zhège jiǔdiàn búdàn fāngbiàn, érqiě piányi
this hotel is <u>not only</u> convenient <u>but also</u> cheap

我们不但要看，而且要帮
wǒmen búdàn yàokàn, érqiě yào bāng
(*lit.* we should <u>not only</u> watch <u>but also</u> help)
we shouldn't just watch, we should help

4 一边 **yìbiān ...** 一边 **yìbiān** (while, as, at the same time)

他们喜欢一边吃饭，一边看电视
tāmen xǐhuān yìbiān chīfàn, yìbiān kàn diànshì
they like to have their meal <u>while</u> watching TV

我一边工作，一边学习
wǒ yìbiān gōngzuò, yìbiān xuéxí
I work and study <u>at the same time</u>

C COHESIVE CONJUNCTIONS

Cohesive conjunctions are used in Chinese to link two separate clauses by indicating the relationship between them. The most common cohesive conjunctions are given below. Cohesive conjunctions generally appear at the head of the clause to which they refer.

1 因此 **yīncǐ** (therefore, hence, thus, consequently, so)

他昨天生病，因此没上学
tā zuótiān shēngbìng, yīncǐ méi shàngxué
he was ill yesterday, <u>so</u> didn't go to school

他非常友好，因此大家都喜欢他
tā fēicháng yǒuhǎo, yīncǐ dàjiā dōu xǐhuān tā
he's very friendly, <u>hence</u> everyone likes him

2 可是 **kěshì**, 但是 **dànshì** and 不过 **búguò** (but, yet, however, nevertheless)

他看了两遍，可是还是看不懂
tā kàn-le liǎng biàn, kěshì háishì kànbùdǒng
he had seen it twice, <u>yet</u> still didn't understand

最近雨下得很多，但是不冷
zuìjìn yǔ xiàde hěn duō, dànshì bù lěng
(*lit.* recently it's raining a lot, <u>but</u> it's not cold)
it's raining a lot recently, but it's not cold

我哥哥和弟弟都喜欢打网球，不过我比较喜欢游泳
wǒ gēge hé dìdi dōu xǐhuān dǎ wǎngqiú, búguò wǒ bǐjiào xǐhuān
   yóuyǒng
my older and younger brothers like to play tennis, <u>however</u> I prefer
   swimming

3 否则 **fǒuzé** and 要不然 **yàobùrán** (otherwise, if not, or else)

快走，否则要迟到了！
kuài zǒu, fǒuzé yào chídào le!
hurry, <u>otherwise</u> we'll be late!

我们要请他，要不然他会不高兴
wǒmen yào qǐng tā, yàobùrán tā huì bù gāoxìng
we have to invite him, <u>or else</u> he'll be offended

4 反而 **fǎnér** (on the contrary, on the other hand)

爱丁堡在伦敦的北面，反而比伦敦热
Àidīngbǎo zài Lúndūn de běimiàn, fǎnér bǐ Lúndūn rè
Edinburgh is north of London, but <u>contrary</u> to what one might think,
   it's warmer

5 Time-linking conjunctions

The time-linking conjunctions 的时候 de shíhòu (when) and 然后
ránhòu (then, afterwards) are used to show that two clauses occur in

relation to each other. Note that unlike in English, 的时候 de shíhòu appears at the end of the clause to which it refers:

> 我吃饭的时候，他在睡觉
> wǒ chīfàn <u>de shíhòu</u>, tā zài shuìjiào
> (*lit.* I was eating <u>when</u>, he was sleeping)
> he was sleeping while I was eating

> 先到的是秋天，然后是冬天
> xiān dào de shì qiūtiān, <u>ránhòu</u> shì dōngtiān
> first comes autumn, <u>then</u> winter

6 Inference conjunctions

The common inference conjunctions, 就 jiù (then) and 还是 háishì (still), are used before a verb to show that the speaker or writer infers or deduces something in the second clause, based on the evidence of the first clause:

> 你去，我就去
> nǐ qù, wǒ <u>jiù</u> qù
> if you go, <u>then</u> I'll go

> 他没说，我们还是看出来了
> tā méi shuō, wǒmen <u>háishì</u> kànchūlái le
> even though he didn't mention it, we can <u>still</u> tell

7 Listing conjunctions

The listing conjunctions 先 xiān ... 再 zài (first ... then), 先 xiān ... 然后 ránhòu (first ... after that) and 一 yí ... 就 jiù (as soon as) are used to link two actions that follow on from one another. Each part of the conjunction appears immediately before a verb. It is important to remember that any construction with 再 zài can only be used for future events or to plan an event, whereas constructions with 然后 ránhòu can be used in any tense:

> 你先走，我再走
> nǐ <u>xiān</u> zǒu, wǒ <u>zài</u> zǒu
> (*lit.* you <u>first</u> go, I <u>then</u> go)
> you leave first, and then I'll go

她先学了汉语，然后学了法语
tā xiān xué-le Hànyǔ, ránhòu xué-le Fǎyǔ
<u>first</u> she studied Chinese, <u>after that</u> she studied French

她先学汉语，然后学法语
tā xiān xué Hànyǔ, ránhòu xué Fǎyǔ
<u>first</u> she'll study Chinese, <u>then</u> French

他一看到我就跑
tā yí kàndào wǒ jiù pǎo
<u>as soon as</u> he saw me, he ran

8 Single-word listing conjunctions

The listing conjunctions 以前 yǐqián (before), 以后 yǐhòu (after) and
后来 hòulái (then, later) consist of one word only. 以前 yǐqián and 以
后 yǐhòu appear at the end of the clause to which they refer. Note
that the single-word listing conjunctions can be used in the past
tense only:

我来中国以前，没吃过龙眼
wǒ lái Zhōngguó yǐqián, méi chī-guò lóngyǎn
<u>before</u> I came to China, I'd never tasted longgan

他们来了以后，我们都变得更喜欢学中文
tāmen lái-le yǐhòu, wǒmen dōu biàn-de gèng xǐhuān xué Zhōngwén
<u>after</u> they arrived, we were more interested in learning Chinese

他一直喜欢运动，后来当了体育老师
tā yìzhí xǐhuān yùndòng, hòulái dāng-le tǐyù lǎoshī
he had always liked sports, <u>later</u> he became a PE teacher

D SUBORDINATING CONJUNCTIONS

Like cohesive conjunctions (*see* **Section C**), subordinating
conjunctions are used to indicate the relationship between
two clauses in Chinese. However, clauses with a subordinating
conjunction are generally used to justify or give a reason for an
action and must be composed of two parts.

In English, it is sometimes perceived as inappropriate or 'bad style' to begin a sentence with a subordinating conjunction (eg 'because'). However, in Chinese the subordinating clause *must* come before the main clause. The most common subordinating conjunctions are listed below.

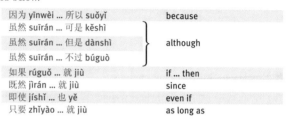

因为 yīnwèi ... 所以 suǒyǐ	because
虽然 suīrán ... 可是 kěshì	
虽然 suīrán ... 但是 dànshì	although
虽然 suīrán ... 不过 búguò	
如果 rúguǒ ... 就 jiù	if ... then
既然 jìrán ... 就 jiù	since
即使 jíshǐ ... 也 yě	even if
只要 zhǐyào ... 就 jiù	as long as

1 因为 **yīnwèi** ... 所以 **suǒyǐ** (because)

因为下雨，所以我没去
yīnwèi xiàyǔ, suǒyǐ wǒ méi qù
(*lit.* <u>because</u> it rained, <u>therefore</u> I did not go)
I didn't go because it rained

因为他很喜欢书，所以一共买了五本
yīnwèi tā hěn xǐhuān shū, suǒyǐ yígòng mǎi-le wǔ běn
(*lit.* <u>because</u> he likes books, <u>therefore</u> he bought five)
because he likes books, he bought five

2 虽然 **suīrán** ... 可是 **kěshì**/但是 **dànshì**/不过 **búguò** (although)

These constructions can be used interchangeably to express 'although'. Note that 虽然 suīrán can appear either before or after the subject of the sentence without changing the meaning:

他虽然很努力，可是考试没有及格
tā suīrán hěn nǔlì, kěshì kǎoshì méiyǒu jígé
(*lit.* he <u>although</u> worked hard, <u>but</u> he failed the exam)
although he worked hard, he failed the exam

虽然他很努力, 可是考试没有及格
suīrán tā hěn nǔlì, kěshì kǎoshì méiyǒu jígé
(*lit.* although he worked hard, but he failed the exam)
although he worked hard, he failed the exam

3 如果 rúguǒ ... 就 jiù (if ... then)

This construction carries the meaning 'provided that ... then' and can be used to express the conditional tense. Note that 如果 rúguǒ appears before the subject of the first clause, whilst 就 jiù always appears *after* the subject of the second clause:

如果你今天来我家, (你)就会看到我的小狗
rúguǒ nǐ jīntiān lái wǒ jiā, (nǐ) jiù huì kàndào wǒde xiǎogǒu
if you come to my house today, then you will be able to see my little dog

如果你去, 我就去
rúguǒ nǐ qù, wǒ jiù qù
if you go, then I'll go

4 既然 jìrán ... 就 jiù (since)

你既然不喜欢, (你)就不要买
nǐ jìrán bù xǐhuān, (nǐ) jiù bú yào mǎi
since you don't like it, you shouldn't buy it

既然火车晚了, 我们就去喝咖啡吧!
jìrán huǒchē wǎn le, wǒmen jiù qù hē kāfēi ba!
now that the train is late, let's go and have a coffee!

5 即使 jíshǐ ... 也 yě (even if ...)

即使你不去, 我也会去
jíshǐ nǐ bú qù, wǒ yě huì qù
even if you are not going, I will be going

即使明天下雨, 演唱会也要继续进行
jíshǐ míngtiān xiàyǔ, yǎnchànghuì yě yào jìxù jìnxíng
even if it should rain, the concert will go ahead

6 只要 zhǐyào ... 就 jiù (as long as)

只要你来，我就请你吃饭
zhǐyào nǐ lái, wǒ jiù qǐng nǐ chīfàn
as long as you come, I'll treat you to a meal

只要你做完功课就可以走
zhǐyào nǐ zuòwán gōngkè jiù kěyǐ zǒu
you may go provided your homework is complete

7 'Unless, only if'

The following three constructions can be used when an action in the second clause will only take place if a condition in the first clause is fulfilled.

除非 chúfēi ... 才 cái

除非 chúfēi ... 要不然 yàobùrán ... 就 jiù

只有 zhǐyǒu ... 才 cái

除非你去，我才去
chúfēi nǐ qù, wǒ cái qù
(*lit.* only if you go, then I'll go)
I'll only go if you go/I won't go unless you go

除非你去，要不然我就不去
chúfēi nǐ qù, yàobùrán wǒ jiù bú qù
(*lit.* unless you go, or else I'll not go)
I'll only go if you go/I won't go unless you go

只有你去，我才去
zhǐyǒu nǐ qù, wǒ cái qù
(*lit.* only if you go, then I'll go)
I'll only go if you go/I won't go unless you go

Note that where in English a negative is always used in a sentence with 'unless' (I won't go unless you go), in Chinese 才 cái already carries the negative.

14 NUMBERS AND QUANTITY

A CARDINAL NUMBERS

These are the standard number forms like 'one', 'two', 'ten', as opposed to ordinal numbers (*see* page 119).

1 Counting to ten

0	零 líng		
1	一 yī	6	六 liù
2	二 èr	7	七 qī
3	三 sān	8	八 bā
4	四 sì	9	九 jiǔ
5	五 wǔ	10	十 shí

Note that o is an informal way to represent zero, in place of 零 líng.

> ### Note
>
> In Chinese, the number two is a 'double agent'. It is represented by 二 èr when it is used as a numeral, but when it appears before a measure word, it becomes 两 liǎng (*see also* pages 124-5):
>
> 两个学生   两只猫
> liǎng gè xuésheng   liǎng zhī māo
> <u>two</u> students   <u>two</u> cats

2 Counting beyond ten

11	十一 shí yī	21	二十一 èr shí yī
12	十二 shí èr	22	二十二 èr shí èr
13	十三 shí sān	30	三十 sān shí
14	十四 shí sì	40	四十 sì shí
15	十五 shí wǔ	50	五十 wǔ shí
16	十六 shí liù	60	六十 liù shí
17	十七 shí qī	70	七十 qī shí
18	十八 shí bā	80	八十 bā shí
19	十九 shí jiǔ	90	九十 jiǔ shí
20	二十 èr shí	100	一百 yì bǎi

3 Counting beyond one hundred

1,000	一千 yì qiān
10,000	一万 yì wàn
100,000	十万 shí wàn
1,000,000	一百万 yì bǎi wàn
10,000,000	一千万 yì qiān wàn
100,000,000	亿 yì
1,000,000,000	十亿 shí yì

Some examples:

五百二十三
wǔ bǎi èr shí sān
523

一千零八
yì qiān líng bā
1,008

一万四千六百三十八
yí wàn sì qiān liù bǎi sān shí bā
14,638

十五万三千七百六十五
shí wǔ wàn sān qiān qī bǎi liù shí wǔ
153,765

> ### Note
>
> While numbers in the twenties are formed using 二 èr, all
> subsequent numbers beginning with the number two may also
> be formed using 两 liǎng. For example:
>
> | 20 | 二十 èr shí |
> |----|-----------|
> | 200 | 两百 liǎng bǎi |
> | 2,000 | 两千 liǎng qiān |
> | 20,000 | 两万 liǎng wàn |

4 Reading numbers

When reading a sequence of numbers, such as a telephone number
or a year, simply say each digit individually:

> líng yī sān yī sān yī èr èr èr líng líng
> 0131 312 2200
>
> èr líng líng bā (nián)
> (the year) 2008

B ORDINAL NUMBERS

Ordinal numbers are used to express order: 'first', 'second', 'tenth' *etc.*
Place 第 dì before the numeral to form an ordinal number:

first/1st	第一 dì yī
second/2nd	第二 dì èr
third/3rd	第三 dì sān
tenth/10th	第十 dì shí

When using an ordinal number with a noun, a measure word is required. For example:

第一个运动员
dì yí ge yùndòngyuán
the first athlete

第二本词典
dì èr <u>běn</u> cídiǎn
the second dictionary

In some instances, ordinal numbers are not required in Chinese where they would be in English. Instead, a cardinal number can be used without a measure word. Because there is no measure word, ordinal numbers formed in this way will not be confused with plural nouns:

三班
sān bān
(*lit.* <u>three</u> class)
the <u>third</u> class (*school*)

二楼
èr lóu
(*lit.* <u>two</u> floor)
the <u>first</u> floor

Note that 'ground floor' in British English is translated as 一楼 yì lóu (*lit.* one floor) and 'first floor' is translated as 二楼 èr lóu (*lit.* two floor).

C MATHEMATICAL EXPRESSIONS

1 Arithmetic

plus/to add	加 jiā
minus/to subtract	减 jiǎn
multiplied by/to multiply	乘(以) chéng(yǐ)
divided by/to divide	除以 chúyǐ
equals/to be equal to	等于 děngyú

八加五等于十三
bā jiā wǔ děngyú shí sān
8 + 5 = 13

七减二等于五
qī jiǎn èr děngyú wǔ
7 − 2 = 5

八乘(以)八等于六十四
bā chéng(yǐ) bā děngyú liù shí sì
8 x 8 = 64

二十七除以九等于三
èr shi qī chúyǐ jiǔ děngyú sān
27 ÷ 9 = 3

2 Decimals

The decimal point is expressed as 点 diǎn:

二十三点八
èr shí sān diǎn bā
23.8

3 Fractions

Fractions can be expressed by the construction 'denominator + 分之 fēn zhī + numerator':

三分之二
sān fēn zhī èr
2/3

十分之一
shí fēn zhī yī
1/10

Note that 分 fēn means 'part' and 之 zhī means 'of'.

4 Percentages

Percentages are expressed using '百 bǎi (hundred) + 分之 fēn zhī + percentage':

百分之十五
bǎi fēn zhī shí wǔ
15%

百分之九十五
bǎi fēn zhī jiǔ shí wǔ
95%

D APPROXIMATE NUMBERS

1 差不多 chàbùduō, 左右 zuǒyòu and 上下 shàngxià

Approximate numbers can be expressed using the words 差不多 chàbùduō (around), 左右 zuǒyòu (approximately) and 上下 shàngxià (about):

> 差不多五十岁
> chàbùduō wǔ shí suì
> <u>around</u> 50 years old

> 八千上下
> bā qiān <u>shàngxià</u>
> (*lit.* <u>above and below</u> eight thousand)
> about eight thousand

> 三十左右
> sān shí <u>zuǒyòu</u>
> (*lit.* <u>to the left and right of</u> thirty)
> approximately thirty

Note that 差不多 chàbùduō is placed *before* the number, whereas 左右 zuǒyòu and 上下 shàngxià appear *after* the number.

2 The enumerative comma

A range of numbers can be expressed in Chinese using the enumerative comma (*see also* **page 21**):

> 七、八十
> qī, bā shí
> (*lit.* <u>seven, eight</u> ten)
> seventy to eighty

> 五、六百人
> wǔ, liù bǎi rén
> (*lit.* <u>five, six</u> hundred people)
> five to six hundred people

3 几 jǐ

The determiner 几 jǐ (a few/several) may be used before 十 shí (ten), 百 bǎi (hundred), 千 qiān (thousand), 万 wàn (ten thousand) and 亿 yì (hundred million) to express 'tens of...', 'hundreds of...' *etc*:

几百种茶
jǐ bǎi zhǒng chá
<u>hundreds</u> of types of tea

4 多 duō

The adjective 多 duō (more than) can be used after 十 shí, 百 bǎi, 千 qiān, 万 wàn or 亿 yì to indicate an approximate number greater than the specified one:

十多岁
shí <u>duō</u> suì
<u>more than</u> ten years of age

一千多人
yì qiān <u>duō</u> rén
<u>over</u> a thousand people

5 以上 yǐshàng and 以下 yǐxià

以上 yǐshàng (or more) can be used to indicate a value equal to or greater than the specified number. 以下 yǐxià (or less) indicates a value less than or equal to the specified number. Both appear *after* the number:

三十以上
sān shí <u>yǐshàng</u>
thirty <u>or more</u>

六十块钱以下
liù shí kuài qián <u>yǐxià</u>
sixty dollars <u>or less</u>

6 来 lái

来 lái can be used after 十 shí, 百 bǎi, 千 qiān, 万 wàn or 亿 yì to show approximation:

二十来岁
èr shí <u>lái</u> suì
<u>around</u> twenty years old

15 EXPRESSIONS OF QUANTITY

A MEASURE WORDS

In Chinese, nouns cannot be quantified by a numeral alone. A specific measure word must be added between the numeral and the noun. For example:

三个教室
sān ge jiàoshì
three classrooms

The same applies to nouns preceded by the demonstrative pronouns 这 zhè (this) and 那 nà (that). For example:

这个演员
zhè ge yǎnyuán
this actor

For more on demonstrative pronouns, see also pages 50-1.

1 The common 个 ge

Measure words are so important in Chinese that there are well over a hundred in use. However, 个 ge is the most common measure word and can be used as a substitute where the actual measure word is unknown.

一个人
yí ge rén
one person

三个国家
sān ge guójiā
three countries

两个哥哥
liǎng ge gēge
two brothers

四个儿子
sì ge érzi
four sons

五个汉堡包
wǔ ge hànbǎobao
five hamburgers

Note that when 二 èr (two) appears before a measure word, it becomes 两 liǎng.

2 Types of measure words

The measure word associated with a particular noun depends on the general meaning or characteristics of that noun. Measure words can be broadly grouped into the following two types:

a) Measure words used in a similar way in English

For example:

八瓶水
bā píng shuǐ
eight bottles of water

Measure word	*Equivalent*	*Example*
杯 bēi	cup of, glass of, mug of	一杯咖啡 yì bēi kāfēi a mug of coffee
瓶 píng	bottle of	三瓶啤酒 sān píng píjiǔ three bottles of beer
包 bāo	packet of	一包糖 yì bāo táng a packet of sweets
块 kuài	piece of	一块蛋糕 yí kuài dàngāo a piece of cake
排 pái	row of/line of	九排人 jiǔ pái rén nine rows of people

| 双 shuāng | pair of | 一双筷子
yì shuāng kuàizi
a <u>pair of</u> chopsticks |
| 盒 hé | box of | 一盒巧克力
yì hé qiǎokèlì
a <u>box of</u> chocolates |

b) Measure words sometimes used or not required in English
For example:

Measure word	*Used with*	*Example*
把 bǎ	objects held in the hand	一把刀 yì bǎ dāo <u>one/a</u> knife
只 zhī	animals, birds and insects	一只猪 yì zhī zhū <u>one/a</u> pig
	one of a pair	一只手 yì zhī shǒu <u>one/a</u> hand
	utensils	一只锅 yì zhī guō <u>one/a</u> wok
条 tiáo	long, narrow objects	这条裤子 zhè tiáo kùzi <u>these</u> trousers
张 zhāng	flat surfaces	一张床 yì zhāng chuáng <u>one/a</u> bed
根 gēn	thin, slender objects	一根草 yì gēn cǎo <u>one/a</u> blade of grass
支 zhī	fairly long, stick-like objects	一支烟 yì zhī yān <u>one/a</u> cigarette

串 chuàn	items joined together, eg by a string	一串葡萄 yí chuàn pútao a bunch of grapes
颗 kē	small objects or objects which appear small	一颗星 yì kē xīng one/a star
家 jiā	shops, restaurants and hospitals	一家餐馆 yì jiā cānguǎn one/a restaurant
户 hù	households	一户人家 yí hù rénjiā one/a household
间 jiān	rooms	一间厨房 yì jiān chúfáng one/a kitchen
件 jiàn	items of clothing (generally for the upper body)	一件衬衫 yí jiàn chènshān one/a shirt
	matters, affairs	一件事 yí jiàn shì one/a matter
种 zhǒng	types of	一种水果 yì zhǒng shuǐguǒ one/a type of fruit
封 fēng	letters, mail	一封信 yì fēng xìn one/a letter
台 tái	fairly large electrical items	一台洗衣机 yì tái xǐyījī one/a washing machine
辆 liàng	wheeled vehicles	一辆车 yí liàng chē one/a car

架 jià	machinery, vehicles (not considered wheeled)	一架飞机 yí jià fēijī <u>one</u>/<u>an</u> aeroplane
位 wèi	people (a polite measure word to replace 个 ge)	一位客人 yí wèi kèrén <u>one</u>/<u>a</u> visitor
名 míng	people, members of a particular social group	一名大学教师 yì míng dàxué jiàoshī <u>one</u>/<u>a</u> university teacher

3 Verbal measure words

Measure words must also be used with verbs when indicating the frequency of an action or occurrence. The numeral and measure word follow the verb:

Measure word	*Used for*	*Example*
次 cì	frequencies of an action, whether completed or not	看过一次 kàn-guò yí cì seen it <u>once</u>
回 huí	occurrences (similar to, but more colloquial than 次 cì)	看了两回 kàn le liǎng <u>huí</u> seen it <u>twice</u>
趟 tàng	trips, journeys	他去了三趟 tā qù-le sān <u>tàng</u> he went on three trips
场 chǎng	durations of events	我昨天晚上去看了一场戏 wǒ zuótiān wǎnshàng qù kàn-leyì <u>chǎng</u> xì I went to see <u>one</u>/<u>a</u> performance
顿 dùn	short, unrepeated actions	吃一顿饭 chī yí <u>dùn</u> fàn to eat <u>one</u>/<u>a</u> meal

4 Nouns which do not require a measure word

Some single-syllable nouns in Chinese have measure words 'built in' and need only be preceded by a numeral:

Noun	Equivalent	Example
天 tiān	day	三天 sān tiān three days
岁 suì	years of age	八十八岁 bā shí bā suì eighty-eight years of age
年 nián	year	一年 yì nián one year
国 guó	nation	六国 liù guó six nations

5 Standard units of measurement

Standard units of measurement act as measure words and need only be preceded by a numeral:

Units of currency

镑 bàng	pounds sterling	二十镑 èr shí bàng 20 pounds
便士 biànshi	penny/pence	六便士 liu biànshi 6 pence
块 kuài	RMB dollar *(informal)*	九块(钱) jiǔ kuài (qián) 9 dollars
元 yuàn	RMB dollar *(formal)*	五十元 wǔ shí yuàn 50 dollars

EXPRESSIONS OF QUANTITY

分 fēn	cent	七分(钱) qī fēn (qián) 7 <u>cents</u>
角 jiǎo	units of 10 cents	五角 wǔ jiǎo 50 <u>cents</u>
毛 máo	units of 10 cents *(informal)*	三毛 sān máo 30 <u>cents</u>

Units of weight

公斤 gōngjīn	kilogram	八十公斤 bā shí gōngjīn 80 <u>kg</u>
克 kè	gram	五十克 wǔ shí <u>kè</u> 50 <u>g</u>
磅 bàng	pound (lb)	七十八磅 qī shí bā <u>bàng</u> 78 <u>lbs</u>

Units of length/distance

公里 gōnglǐ	kilometre	十公里 shí gōnglǐ 10 <u>km</u>
公尺 gōngchǐ	metre	一百公尺 yì bǎi gōngchǐ 100 <u>m</u>
公分 gōngfēn	centimetre	五公分 wǔ gōngfēn 5 <u>cm</u>
尺 chǐ	foot	六尺 liù <u>chǐ</u> 6 <u>feet</u>
寸 cùn	inch	一寸 yí cùn 1 <u>inch</u>

B OTHER EXPRESSIONS OF QUANTITY

1 Half

半 bàn (half) behaves in the same way as a numeral before a noun and must be followed by a measure word appropriate to the noun:

> 半个苹果
> bàn ge píngguǒ
> <u>half</u> an apple

However, when 半 bàn is used to express '... and a half', the construction changes to 'number + measure word + 半 bàn + noun'.

> 一个半苹果
> yí ge <u>bàn</u> píngguǒ
> one <u>and a half</u> apples

2 Indefinite measure words

一些 yìxiē (some) and 一点 yìdiǎn (a bit, a little) are measure words used to refer to an indefinite number or amount. The first syllable of both words is always 一 yì (one), it can never be replaced with another numeral.

一些学生	*never*	三些学生
yìxiē xuésheng		sānxiē xuésheng
<u>some</u> students		
多一点		少一点
duō yìdiǎn		shǎo yìdiǎn
<u>a bit</u> more		<u>a little</u> less

3 Adjectives of quantity

There are some set expressions of quantity in Chinese. These appear directly before the noun and do not require a measure word:

多 duō many	太多 tài duō too many
少 shǎo few/little	太少 tài shǎo too few/little
够 gòu enough	不够 bú gòu not enough

16 EXPRESSIONS OF TIME

A THE DATE

Dates are always expressed in the order 年 nián (year), 月 yuè (month), 日 rì (day):

二零零八年四月五日
èr líng líng bā nián sì yuè wǔ rì
5 April 2008

1 Years

Years are expressed by inserting 年 nián (year) after the single digits that make up that year:

一九七二年
yī jiǔ qī èr <u>nián</u>
(*lit.* one nine seven two year)
1972

二零零八年
èr líng líng bā <u>nián</u>
2008

一九九七年
yī jiǔ jiǔ qī <u>nián</u>
1997

2 Months

Months are expressed by inserting the word 月 yuè (month) after the number that corresponds to the month, beginning with 1 for January.

January	一月 yí yuè	April	四月 sì yuè
February	二月 èr yuè	May	五月 wǔ yuè
March	三月 sān yuè	June	六月 liù yuè

July	七月 qī yuè	October	十月 shí yuè
August	八月 bā yuè	November	十一月 shí-yī yuè
September	九月 jiǔ yuè	December	十二月 shí-èr yuè

3 Dates

The date of the month is expressed by inserting 号 hào or 日 rì (day) after the number corresponding to the date. Note that 号 hào is more commonly used in spoken Chinese, and 日 rì in written Chinese.

一月一号
yí yuè yí hào
1 January

六月四号
liù yuè sì hào
4 June

九月十三日
jiǔ yuè shí-sān rì
13 September

十二月二十五日
shí-èr yuè èr-shí-wǔ rì
25 December

4 Days of the week

To express the days of the week from Monday to Saturday, the numbers 1 to 6 must follow 星期 xīngqī or 周 zhōu (week), beginning with 1 for Monday. Note that while 星期 xīngqī is commonly used in spoken Chinese, 周 zhōu is the standard form in written Chinese.

Monday	星期一 xīngqīyī
	周一 zhōuyī
Tuesday	星期二 xīngqīèr
	周二 zhōuèr
Wednesday	星期三 xīngqīsān
	周三 zhōusān
Thursday	星期四 xīngqīsì
	周四 zhōusì
Friday	星期五 xīngqīwǔ
	周五 zhōuwǔ

Saturday	星期六 xīngqīliù
	周六 zhōuliù
Sunday	星期天 xīngqītiān
	周日 zhōurì

 B THE TIME

1 Full hours

To express full hours, 点 diǎn or 点钟 diǎnzhōng, roughly translated as 'o'clock', are used:

七点	九点钟
qī <u>diǎn</u>	jiǔ <u>diǎnzhōng</u>
7 <u>o'clock</u>	9 <u>o'clock</u>

2 Half hours

To express half hours, 点 diǎn and 半 bàn (half) are used:

八点半	三点半
bā diǎn <u>bàn</u>	sān diǎn <u>bàn</u>
<u>half past</u> eight	<u>half past</u> three

3 Quarter hours

To express quarter hours, 点 diǎn and 刻 kè (quarter) are used:

七点一刻	九点三刻
qī diǎn yí <u>kè</u>	jiǔ diǎn sān <u>kè</u>
a <u>quarter past</u> seven	(*lit.* three quarters past nine)
	a <u>quarter to</u> ten

4 Minutes

Minutes *past* the hour are expressed using 分 fēn (minute):

七点十分	九点二十五分
qī diǎn shí <u>fēn</u>	jiǔ diǎn èr shí wǔ <u>fēn</u>
ten (<u>minutes</u>) past seven	twenty (<u>minutes</u>) past nine

Note that 零 líng (zero) is added when the number of minutes after the hour is less than 10:

七点零五分
qī diǎn líng wǔ fēn
five (minutes) past seven

Minutes *to* the hour are expressed using 分 fēn and 差 chà (to be short of), which can come before or after 点 diǎn:

差十分九点
<u>chà</u> shí fēn jiǔ diǎn
ten <u>to</u> nine

九点差十分
jiǔ diǎn <u>chà</u> shí fēn
ten <u>to</u> nine

5 Other expressions

a) 'am' and 'pm'

To express 'am' and 'pm' in Chinese, 早上 zǎoshàng (early morning), 上午 shàngwǔ (morning), 下午 xiàwǔ (afternoon) and 晚上 wǎnshàng (evening) are used as appropriate:

早上七点钟
<u>zǎoshàng</u> qī diǎnzhōng
7 am

上午十点半
<u>shàngwǔ</u> shí diǎn bàn
10.30 am

下午三点一刻
<u>xiàwǔ</u> sān diǎn yí kè
3.15 pm

晚上十点三十五分
<u>wǎnshàng</u> shí diǎn sān-shí-wǔ fēn
10.35 pm

b) Past, present and future

The following are common expressions of time:
❏ with 天 tiān (day)

yesterday	昨天 zuótiān
the day before yesterday	前天 qiántiān
three days ago	大前天 dà qiántiān
today	今天 jīntiān
tomorrow	明天 míngtiān

the day after tomorrow	后天 hòutiān
in three days' time	大后天 dà hòutiān

❏ with 星期 xīngqī (week) and 月 yuè (month)

last week	上(个)星期 shàng (ge) xīngqī
last month	上个月 shàng ge yuè
this week	这(个)星期 zhè (ge) xīngqī
this month	这个月 zhè ge yuè
next week	下(个)星期 xià (ge) xīngqī
next month	下(个)月 xià (ge) yuè
in two weeks' time	下下(个)星期 xià xià (ge) xīngqī
in two months' time	下下个月 xià xià ge yuè

❏ with 年 nián (year)

last year	去年 qùnián
the year before last	前年 qiánnián
this year	今年 jīnnián
next year	明年 míngnián
the year after next	后年 hòunián

17 COMPARISON

The comparative allows two things, people or actions to be compared. In English the comparative is formed using words such as 'more', 'less' and 'as ... as' or with the comparative forms of adjectives or adverbs, '...er than'. In Chinese, however, adjectives and adverbs do not have comparative forms and instead comparison is generally indicated by the preposition 比 bǐ when positive, or by the negator 没有 méiyǒu when negative.

A POSITIVE COMPARISON

1 Comparing nouns with 比 bǐ

The preposition 比 bǐ (compared with) is used with an adjective to express comparison between two people or things in the construction 'noun + 比 bǐ + noun + adjective'. Note that the person or thing that is bigger, faster, stronger *etc* must come first in the sentence:

> 我比他高
> wǒ bǐ tā gāo
> (*lit*. I <u>compared with</u> him tall)
> I am taller than him

> 这个椅子比那个椅子大
> zhège yǐzi bǐ nàge yǐzi dà
> (*lit*. this chair <u>compared with</u> that chair big)
> this chair is bigger than that chair

2 Comparing actions with 比 **bǐ**

When a comparison is made between two actions, 比 bǐ is used in the construction 'noun + (verb + 得 de) + 比 bǐ + noun + (verb + 得 de) + adverb':

> 他吃得比我(吃得)多
> tā chī-de bǐ wǒ (chī-de) duō
> (*lit.* he eats <u>compared with</u> I [eat] more)
> he eats more than me

> 我(跑得)比他跑得快
> wǒ (pǎo-de) bǐ tā pǎo-de kuài
> (*lit.* I [run] <u>compared with</u> he runs fast)
> I run faster than him

Note that where the same verb is used twice, it is possible to omit it in one instance (shown in brackets).

3 Degrees of comparison with 比 **bǐ**

Adverbs such as 一点 yìdiǎn (a bit), 得多 deduō (much) and 多了 duōle (a lot) may be used *after* an adjective or adverb to indicate degrees of comparison:

> 我比爸爸高多了
> wǒ bǐ bàba gāo duōle
> I'm <u>a lot</u> taller than Dad

> 他吃得比我多一点
> tā chī-de bǐ wǒ duō yìdiǎn
> he eats <u>a bit</u> more than me

> 我比他跑得快得多
> wǒ bǐ tā pǎo-de kuài deduō
> I run <u>much</u> faster than him

The adverb 更 gèng (even more) may be used *before* an adjective or adverb to indicate a much greater degree of comparison:

> 我比爸爸更高
> wǒ bǐ bàba gèng gāo
> I am <u>even</u> taller than Dad

> 我比他跑得更快
> wǒ bǐ tā pǎo-de gèng kuài
> I run <u>even</u> faster than him

When it is clear from the context that a comparison is being made, it is possible to use 更 gèng without 比 bǐ:

他妈妈唱得更好
tā māma chàng-de gèng hǎo
(he sings very well), his mother sings even better

B NEGATIVE COMPARISON

1 Comparing nouns with 没有 méiyǒu

In a similar way to 比 bǐ (*see* Section A), 没有 méiyǒu (not have) may be used in the construction 'noun + 没有 méiyǒu + noun + adjective' to make comparisons between two nouns, where in English the construction 'not as ... as' would be used:

茶没有咖啡贵
chá <u>méiyǒu</u> kāfēi guì
(*lit.* tea <u>not as</u> coffee expensive)
tea is not as expensive as coffee

我的汽车没有你的大
wǒde qìchē <u>méiyǒu</u> nǐde dà
(*lit.* my car <u>not as</u> yours big)
my car isn't as big as yours

2 Comparing actions with 没有 méiyǒu

When a comparison is made between two actions, 没有 méiyǒu may be used in the construction 'noun + (verb + 得 de) + 没有 méiyǒu + noun + (verb + 得 de) + adverb':

我(走得)没有他(走得)快
wǒ (zǒu-de) <u>méiyǒu</u> tā (zǒu-de) kuài
(*lit.* I walk <u>not as</u> he walks fast)
I don't walk as fast as him

Note that where the same verb is used twice, it is possible to omit it in one instance (shown in brackets).

3 Intensifying comparisons with 没有 méiyǒu

The adverb 那么 nàme can be placed in front of an adjective or
adverb to intensify a comparison with 没有 méiyǒu:

我没有他高　　　　　　　　　　　　我没有他那么高
wǒ <u>méiyǒu</u> tā gāo　　　　→　　　wǒ <u>méiyǒu</u> tā <u>nàme</u> gāo
I'm <u>not as</u> tall as him　　　　　　I'm <u>in no way as</u> tall as him

C SIMILARITY

1 Positive similarity

一样 yíyàng (the same) is often used to express similarity in the
construction 'noun + 跟 gēn (and) + noun + 一样 yíyàng':

你的玩具跟我的玩具一样
nǐde wánjù gēn wǒde wánjù yíyàng
(*lit.* your toys and my toys <u>the same</u>)
your toys are the same as mine

2 Negative similarity

To express 'not the same as', the negator 不 bù is used before
一样 yíyàng:

中国面条跟意大利面不一样
Zhōngguó miàntiáo gēn Yìdàlì miàn <u>bù</u> yíyàng
(*lit.* Chinese noodles and Italian spaghetti <u>not the same</u>)
Chinese noodles are not the same as Italian spaghetti

3 Specific similarity

To express a specific type of similarity, an adjective may be added
after the construction 'noun + 跟 gēn (and) + noun + 一样 yíyàng':

他的汉语跟法语一样好
tāde Hànyǔ gēn Fǎyǔ <u>yíyàng hǎo</u>
(*lit.* his Chinese and French <u>the same good</u>)
his Chinese and French are just as good (as each other)

日本笔跟德国笔一样贵
Rìběn bǐ gēn Déguó bǐ yíyàng guì
(*lit.* Japanese pens and German pens <u>the same expensive</u>)
Japanese pens and German pens are just as expensive (as each other)

4 Comparing similar actions

When used to compare the similarity of two actions, the construction 'noun + (verb + 得 de) + 跟 gēn + noun + (verb + 得 de) + 一样 yíyàng + adverb' can be used:

我(吃得)跟他(吃得)一样快
wǒ (chī-de) gēn tā (chī-de) yíyàng kuài
(*lit.* I eat and he eats <u>the same quickly</u>)
I eat as quickly as him

Note that where the same verb is used twice, it is possible to omit it in one instance (shown in brackets).

 SUPERLATIVE

The superlative is used to express 'the most...' or 'the ...est'. In Chinese, the superlative can be expressed using the adverb 最 zuì (the most).

1 Comparing nouns with 最 zuì

The superlative can be expressed using the construction 'noun + 最 zuì + adjective'.

他最高
tā zuì gāo
(*lit.* he <u>the most</u> tall)
he is the tallest

他的头发最长
tāde tóufa <u>zuì</u> cháng
(*lit.* his hair <u>the most</u> long)
his hair is the longest

2 Comparing actions with 最 zuì

When the superlative relates to actions, the construction 'verb + 得 de + 最 zuì + adverb' is used:

他唱得最好听
tā chàng-de <u>zuì hǎotīng</u>
he sang <u>the most beautifully</u>

他跑得最慢
tā pǎo-de <u>zuì màn</u>
he ran <u>the most slowly</u>

 E CONSTRUCTIONS WITH 越 YUÈ … 越 YUÈ

To indicate a gradual change, the construction 越 yuè … 越 yuè (more and more; the more … the more) can be used in several ways.

1 越来越 yuèláiyuè + adjective

This construction is used to indicate that a noun is 'becoming more and more …':

他的中文越来越好了
tāde Zhōngwén <u>yuèláiyuè</u> hǎo le
his Chinese is <u>getting</u> better and better

天越来越冷了
tiān <u>yuèláiyuè</u> lěng le
the weather is <u>getting</u> colder and colder

Note that the aspect marker 了 le indicates the change in condition (*see also* pages 81-3).

2 Verb + 得 **de** + 越来越 **yuèláiyuè** + adverb

This construction is used to indicate that an action is 'becoming more and more...':

> 她游得越来越快
> tā yóu-de <u>yuèláiyuè</u> kuài
> she swam <u>more and more</u> quickly

3 越来越 **yuèláiyuè** + 喜欢 **xǐhuān** (to like) + verb

> 我越来越喜欢骑车了
> wǒ <u>yuèláiyuè</u> xǐhuān qíchē le
> (*lit.* I <u>more and more</u> like riding bicycle)
> I like cycling more and more

The negator 不 **bù** can be placed before 喜欢 **xǐhuān** (to like) to indicate 'less and less':

> 她越来越不喜欢说话了
> tā <u>yuèláiyuè</u> bù xǐhuān shuōhuà le
> (*lit.* she <u>more and more</u> dislikes talking)
> she likes talking less and less

4 越 **yuè** + adjective + 越 **yuè** + adjective

This construction relates two adjectives to express 'the more ... the ...er':

> 越多越好!
> <u>yuè</u> duō <u>yuè</u> hǎo!
> <u>the more the</u> better

> 越大越漂亮
> <u>yuè</u> dà <u>yuè</u> piàoliàng
> (*lit.* <u>the more</u> big <u>the more</u> pretty)
> the bigger the prettier

5 越 **yuè** + verb + 越 **yuè** + verb/adverb

This construction links a verb to another verb or adverb to express 'the more ... the ...er':

他越说越高兴
tā <u>yuè</u> shuō <u>yuè</u> gāoxìng
<u>the more</u> he spoke, <u>the</u> happi<u>er</u> he became

妈妈越走越快
Māma <u>yuè</u> zǒu <u>yuè</u> kuài
<u>the more</u> Mother walked, <u>the</u> faster she became

6 Noun + 越 **yuè** + verb + noun + 越 **yuè** + verb

This construction is used when the sentence involves two different subjects:

他越说, 我越不想去
tā <u>yuè</u> shuō, wǒ <u>yuè</u> bù xiǎng qù
<u>the more</u> he goes on about it, <u>the more</u> I don't want to go

考试越难, 他越喜欢
kǎoshì <u>yuè</u> nán, tā <u>yuè</u> xǐhuān
<u>the</u> hard<u>er</u> the exam, <u>the more</u> he likes it

18 LOCATION AND DIRECTION

A LOCATION WORDS

In Chinese, basic location words such as 里 lǐ (in) and 外 wài (out) commonly attach to the suffixes 头 tou, 边 biān and 面 miàn. They can therefore exist in two forms (monosyllabic or disyllabic) that have the same meaning but different functions depending on the structure of the sentence. The Form 2 variants can be used interchangeably, but note that those with the suffixes 头 tou and 边 biān are more colloquial. The table below indicates which basic location words take which suffixes.

Form 1 Location word	Form 2 Location word + suffix	Meaning
里 lǐ	里头 lǐtou 里边 lǐbiān 里面 lǐmiàn	in, inside
外 wài	外头 wàitou 外边 wàibiān 外面 wàimiàn	out, outside
上 shàng	上头 shàngtou 上边 shàngbiān 上面 shàngmiàn	on, above
下 xià	下头 xiàtou 下边 xiàbiān 下面 xiàmiàn	under
前 qián	前头 qiántou 前边 qiánbiān 前面 qiánmiàn	in front of

后 hòu	后头 hòutou	behind
	后边 hòubiān	
	后面 hòumiàn	
旁 páng	旁边 pángbiān	next to

The following location words can only have *one* form:

| 对面 duìmiàn | across from, opposite to |
| 中间 zhōngjiān | in between, in the middle |

1 Position of location words

Unlike in English, location words in Chinese can be used *after* a noun. In the following examples, the Form 2 variants may be used interchangeably:

学校里边
xuéxiào <u>lǐbiān</u>
<u>inside</u> the school

教室外头
jiàoshì <u>wàitou</u>
<u>outside</u> the classroom

桌子上面
zhuōzi <u>shàngmiàn</u>
<u>on</u> the table

邮局对面
yóujú <u>duìmiàn</u>
<u>opposite</u> the post office

The position of a location word before or after a noun can affect the meaning. When a location word is used *before* a noun, the noun is the main subject and is modified by the location word. For example:

外头的学校很小
<u>wàitou</u> de xuéxiào hěn xiǎo
schools <u>outside</u> (of a given area) are small

When a location word is used *after* a noun, the location word is the main subject and is modified by the noun. For example:

学校外头有很多花
xuéxiào <u>wàitou</u> yǒu hěn duō huā
<u>outside</u> the school, there are many flowers

2 Use of Form 1 and Form 2 location words

Generally speaking a Form 1 location word must occur with a noun, while a Form 2 location word may be used with a noun or occur independently. For example:

Form 1

学生在教室里
xuéshēng zài jiàoshì lǐ
students are <u>inside</u> the classroom

书架上有很多中文词典
shūjià <u>shàng</u> yǒu hěn duō Zhōngwén cídiǎn
<u>on</u> the bookshelf, there are many Chinese dictionaries

学校前有很多树
xuéxiào <u>qián</u> yǒu hěn duō shù
<u>in front of</u> the school, there are many trees

Form 2

(教室)外头有很多人
(jiàoshì) <u>wàitou</u> yǒu hěn duō rén
<u>outside</u> (the classroom) there are many people

下面是我的房间
<u>xiàmiàn</u> shì wǒde fángjiān
<u>below</u> is my room

前面是我的学校
<u>qiánmiàn</u> shì wǒde xuéxiào
<u>in front</u> is my school

Only one form

邮局在学校和银行中间
yóujú zài xuéxiào hé yínháng <u>zhōngjiān</u>
the post office is <u>in between</u> the school and the bank

B DIRECTION WORDS

The points of the compass can be used with the suffixes 边 biān and 面 miàn to give the following direction words. As with the location words in **Section A**, note that direction words with 边 biān are generally used in a colloquial sense.

east	东边 dōngbiān 东面 dōngmiàn
west	西边 xībiān 西面 xīmiàn
south	南边 nánbiān 南面 nánmiàn
north	北边 běibiān 北面 běimiàn
south-east	东南边 dōngnánbiān 东南面 dōngnánmiàn
north-east	东北边 dōngběibiān 东北面 dōngběimiàn
south-west	西南边 xīnánbiān 西南面 xīnánmiàn
north-west	西北边 xīběibiān 西北面 xīběimiàn

1 Position of direction words

The direction words given in the table above can have different meanings depending on whether they are used before or after a noun. Compare for example:

南边的城市
<u>nánbiān</u> de chéngshì
a city <u>in the south</u>

城市的南边
chéngshì de <u>nánbiān</u>
<u>south of</u> the city

北面的房子
<u>běimiàn</u> de fángzi
houses <u>to the north</u>

房子的北面
fángzi de <u>běimiàn</u>
the <u>north side of</u> the house

2 Expressing location with 在 **zài** (in, at, on)

In Chinese, the preposition 在 zài is commonly used between two locations to express their position in relation to one another. For example:

格拉斯哥在爱丁堡西边
Gélāsīgē <u>zài</u> Àidīngbǎo <u>xībiān</u>
(*lit.* Glasgow <u>at</u> Edinburgh <u>west</u>)
Glasgow is <u>west of</u> Edinburgh

学校在市中心的南面
xuéxiào <u>zài</u> shìzhōngxīn de <u>nánmiàn</u>
the school is <u>in the southside of</u> the city centre

我家在爱丁堡的西北边
wǒ jiā <u>zài</u> Àidīngbǎo de <u>xīběibiān</u>
my home is <u>in the northwest side of</u> Edinburgh

3 Expressing location with 的 **de**

The possessive marker 的 de can be used in the construction '的 de + direction word + verb':

伦敦的西边有很多餐厅
Lúndūn <u>de xībiān</u> yǒu hěn duō cāntīng
(*lit.* London's <u>west side</u> has many restaurants)
there are many restaurants <u>in the west end of</u> London

上海的东边是海
Shànghǎi <u>de dōngbiān</u> shì hǎi
(*lit.* Shanghai's <u>east side</u> is sea)
<u>to the east of</u> Shanghai is the sea

4 Direction word + verb

东南边没下雨
dōngnánbiān méi xiàyǔ
it's not raining <u>in the southeast</u>

北边很漂亮
běibiān hěn piàoliàng
<u>the North</u> is very pretty

5 Use of 部 bù

While the suffixes 边 biān and 面 miàn generally mean 'to the north of', 'to the south of' *etc*, the suffix 部 bù can be loosely translated as 'part' or 'region' and therefore tends to mean 'in the north of', 'in the south of' *etc*. For example, 部 bù is often used when referring to a geographically large region within an area, whilst 边 biān and 面 miàn are frequently used to indicate boundaries or borders:

中国的北部比较冷
Zhōngguó de běibù bǐjiào lěng
in comparison, <u>the northern region of</u> China is colder *(inside the border)*

中国北边比较冷
Zhōngguó běibiān bǐjiào lěng
in comparison, <u>the north side of</u> China is colder *(near the border)*

C EXPRESSIONS OF LOCATION WITH 在 ZÀI AND 有 YǑU

1 Location expressions with 在 zài

In the following constructions, 在 zài functions as both the verb 'to be' and preposition to express 'is in', 'are in', 'is at' and 'are at'.

a) 在 zài + location noun

我爸爸在家
wǒ bàba <u>zài jiā</u>
my father <u>is at home</u>

我妈妈在办公室
wǒ māma <u>zài bàngōngshì</u>
my mother <u>is in the office</u>

b) 在 zài + location noun + location word/direction word

邮局在图书馆南边
yóujú <u>zài túshūguǎn nánbiān</u>
the post office <u>is at the south side of the library</u>

2 Location expressions with 有 **yǒu**

有 yǒu may be used to express 'there is' or 'there are':

教室对面有花园
jiàoshì duìmiàn yǒu huāyuán
(*lit.* classroom opposite <u>there is</u> garden)
opposite the classroom there is a garden

3 Comparing location expressions with 在 **zài** and 有 **yǒu**

The following examples demonstrate the difference in usage between 在 zài and 有 yǒu:

图书馆在学校里
túshūguǎn zài xuéxiào lǐ
(*lit.* library <u>is at</u> school <u>inside</u>)
the library is in the school

学校里有图书馆
xuéxiào lǐ yǒu túshūguǎn
(*lit.* school <u>inside there is</u> library)
there is a library inside the school

学校在商店对面
xuéxiào zài shāngdiàn duìmiàn
(*lit.* school <u>is at</u> shops <u>opposite</u>)
the school is opposite the shops

学校对面有商店
xuéxiào duìmiàn yǒu shāngdiàn
(*lit.* school <u>across from there are</u> shops)
there are shops across from the school

4 Comparing location expressions with 有 **yǒu** and 是 **shì**

The verb 是 shì (to be) may also be used in location expressions. The difference in usage between 是 shì and 有 yǒu is indicated in the following examples:

学校对面有百货商店
xuéxiào duìmiàn yǒu bǎihuò shāngdiàn
(*lit.* school opposite <u>there is</u> department store)
there is a department store opposite the school (*amongst other shops*)

学校对面是百货商店
xuéxiào duìmiàn shì bǎihuò shāngdiàn
(*lit.* school opposite <u>is</u> department store)
the department store is opposite the school

19 LIST OF RADICALS

Every Chinese character contains a radical, or is a radical in its own right. The radical is the 'root' of a character and the basis of its meaning. For example 女 nǚ (woman) is the radical in 妈 mā (mother) and 姐 jiě (elder sister). These characters will both be listed under the radical 女 nǚ in the dictionary. Chinese currently has 214 radicals.

Most Chinese dictionaries list words alphabetically according to their pinyin. However, if you do not know the pinyin for a character or word, then you will need to know the radical in order to look it up in the dictionary's radical index and character index.

Once you have found the radical number, look it up in the character index. This will list all the characters that contain the radical, as well as their pronunciation in pinyin. You can then search for the character in the main dictionary.

The table below lists the numbers of the 214 Chinese radicals, their pinyin transcriptions, English translations and number of strokes. The numbers in the pinyin column indicate tone.

No.	Radical	Pinyin	English	Number of strokes
1	一	yi1	one	1
2	丨	gun3	line	1
3	丶	zhu3	dot	1
4	丿	pie1	slash	1
5	乙	yi3	second	1
6	亅	jue2	hook	1
7	二	er4	two	2
8	亠	tou2	lid	2
9	人	ren2	man	2
10	儿	er2	legs	2

No.	Radical	Pinyin	English	Number of strokes
11	入	ru4	enter	2
12	八	ba1	eight	2
13	冂	jiong3	frontier	2
14	冖	mi4	over	2
15	冫	bing1	ice	2
16	几	ji1	table	2
17	凵	qu3	open box	2
18	刀	dao1	knife	2
19	力	li4	power	2
20	勹	bao1	bundle	2
21	匕	bi3	spoon	2
22	匚	fang1	box	2
23	匸	xi3	box	2
24	十	shi2	ten	2
25	卜	bu3	mysticism	2
26	卩	jie2	seal	2
27	厂	chang3	cliff	2
28	厶	si1	private	2
29	又	you4	again	2
30	口	kou3	mouth	3
31	囗	wei2	enclosure	3
32	土	tu3	earth	3
33	士	shi4	scholar	3
34	夂	sui1	go	3
35	夊	zhi	go slowly	3
36	夕	xi4	evening	3
37	大	da4	big	3
38	女	nü3	woman	3
39	子	zi3	child	3
40	宀	mian2	roof	3
41	寸	cun4	inch	3
42	小	xiao3	small	3

No.	Radical	Pinyin	English	Number of strokes
43	尢	wang1	lame	3
44	尸	shi1	corpse	3
45	屮	che4	sprout	3
46	山	shan1	mountain	3
47	川	chuan1	river	3
48	工	gong1	work	3
49	己	ji3	oneself	3
50	巾	jin1	turban	3
51	干	gan1	dry	3
52	幺	yao1	tiny	3
53	广	guang3	broad	3
54	廴	yin3	stride	3
55	廾	gong3	two hands	3
56	弋	yi4	shoot	3
57	弓	gong1	bow	3
58	彐	ji4	snout	3
59	彡	shan1	bristle	3
60	彳	chi4	step	3
61	心	xin1	heart	4
62	戈	ge1	dagger-axe	4
63	戶	hu4	door	4
64	手	shou3	hand	4
65	支	zhi1	branch	4
66	攴	pu1	pound	4
67	文	wen2	script	4
68	斗	dou3	dipper	4
69	斤	jin1	axe	4
70	方	fang1	square	4
71	无	wu2	without	4
72	日	ri4	sun	4
73	曰	yue1	say	4
74	月	yue4	moon	4
75	木	mu4	tree	4

No.	Radical	Pinyin	English	Number of strokes
76	欠	qian4	yawn	4
77	止	zhi3	stop	4
78	歹	dai3	danger	4
79	殳	shu1	weapon	4
80	毋	mu2	do not	4
81	比	bi3	compare	4
82	毛	mao2	fur	4
83	氏	shi4	clan	4
84	气	qi4	steam	4
85	水	shui3	water	4
86	火	huo3	fire	4
87	爪	zhao3	claw	4
88	父	fu4	father	4
89	爻	yao2	twist	4
90	爿	qiang2	bed	4
91	片	pian4	slice	4
92	牙	ya2	fang	4
93	牛	niu2	cow	4
94	犬	quan3	dog	4
95	玄	xuan2	profound	5
96	玉	yu4	jade	5
97	瓜	gua1	melon	5
98	瓦	wa3	tile	5
99	甘	gan1	sweet	5
100	生	sheng1	life	5
101	用	yong4	use	5
102	田	tian2	field	5
103	疋	pi3	cloth	5
104	疒	chuang2	sickness	5
105	癶	bo1	legs	5
106	白	bai2	white	5
107	皮	pi2	skin	5
108	皿	min3	dish	5

No.	Radical	Pinyin	English	Number of strokes
109	目	mu4	eye	5
110	矛	mao2	spear	5
111	矢	shi3	arrow	5
112	石	shi2	stone	5
113	示	shi4	reveal	5
114	禸	rou3	track	5
115	禾	he2	grain	5
116	穴	xue2	cave	5
117	立	li4	stand	5
118	竹	zhu2	bamboo	6
119	米	mi3	rice	6
120	糸	mi4	silk	6
121	缶	fou3	jar	6
122	网	wang3	net	6
123	羊	yang2	sheep	6
124	羽	yu3	feather	6
125	老	lao3	old	6
126	而	er2	and	6
127	耒	lei3	plough	6
128	耳	er3	ear	6
129	聿	yu4	brush	6
130	肉	rou4	meat	6
131	臣	chen2	minister	6
132	自	zi4	self	6
133	至	zhi4	arrive	6
134	臼	jiu4	mortar	6
135	舌	she2	tongue	6
136	舛	chuan3	opposite	6
137	舟	zhou1	boat	6
138	艮	gen4	stopping	6
139	色	se4	colour	6
140	艸	cao3	grass	6
141	虍	hu3	tiger	6

No.	Radical	Pinyin	English	Number of strokes
142	虫	chong2	insect	6
143	血	xue3	blood	6
144	行	xing2	walk	6
145	衣	yi1	clothes	6
146	西	ya4	west	6
147	見	jian4	see	7
148	角	jiao3	horn	7
149	言	yan2	speech	7
150	谷	gu3	valley	7
151	豆	dou4	bean	7
152	豕	shi3	pig	7
153	豸	zhi4	badger	7
154	貝	bei4	shell	7
155	赤	chi4	red	7
156	走	zou3	run	7
157	足	zu2	foot	7
158	身	shen1	body	7
159	車	che1	cart	7
160	辛	xin1	toil	7
161	辰	chen2	morning	7
162	辵	chuo4	walk	7
163	邑	yi4	city	7
164	酉	you3	wine	7
165	采	cai3	distinguish	7
166	里	li3	village	7
167	金	jin1	gold	8
168	長	chang2	long	8
169	門	men2	gate	8
170	阜	fu4	mound	8
171	隶	dai4	slave	8
172	隹	zhui1	bird	8
173	雨	yu3	rain	8

No.	Radical	Pinyin	English	Number of strokes
174	青	qing1	blue	8
175	非	fei1	wrong	8
176	面	mian4	face	9
177	革	ge2	leather	9
178	韋	wei2	tanned leather	9
179	韭	jiu3	leek	9
180	音	yin1	sound	9
181	頁	ye4	leaf	9
182	風	feng1	wind	9
183	飛	fei1	fly	9
184	食	shi2	eat	9
185	首	shou3	head	9
186	香	xiang1	fragrant	9
187	馬	ma3	horse	10
188	骨	gu3	bone	10
189	高	gao1	tall	10
190	髟	biao1	hair	10
191	鬥	dou4	fight	10
192	鬯	chang4	sacrificial wine	10
193	鬲	li4	cauldron	10
194	鬼	gui3	ghost	10
195	魚	yu2	fish	11
196	鳥	niao3	bird	11
197	鹵	lu3	salt	11
198	鹿	lu4	deer	11
199	麥	mai4	wheat	11
200	麻	ma2	hemp	11
201	黃	huang2	yellow	12
202	黍	shu3	millet	12
203	黑	hei1	black	12
204	黹	zhi3	embroidery	12
205	黽	min3	frog	13
206	鼎	ding3	tripod	13

LIST OF RADICALS

No.	Radical	Pinyin	English	Number of strokes
207	鼓	gu3	drum	13
208	鼠	shu3	rat	13
209	鼻	bi2	nose	14
210	齊	qi2	even	14
211	齒	chi3	tooth	15
212	龍	long2	dragon	16
213	龜	gui1	turtle	16
214	龠	yue4	flute	17

INDEX

a question particle 39
  exclamative 70–2
about to 82
above 146–8
action verbs 7, 79–87
active voice 7
addition 120–1
adjectival stative verbs 7,
    53–5, 73–4, 91
adjectives 7, 22, 52–5
adverbial particle 63
adverbs 7, 53, 56–66
adverbs of degree 56–7, 73
adverbs of doubt and
    certainty 59–60
adverbs of evaluation and
    viewpoint 61
adverbs of frequency 60–1
adverbs of scope 57–8
adverbs of time and duration 58
after 113
all 57, 63
alphabet 13
also 106–10
although 114–5
always 58, 60

a.m. 136
and 106–9
answers 29
anything 64
ànzhào 104
approximate numbers 122–3
arithmetic 120–1
as 110
aspect markers 7, 80–4
associative compounds 17–18
at 33, 96, 99
attributive adjectives 52–3
auxiliaries *see* modal verbs

bǎ 84–7
ba question particle 38
  with imperatives 67–9
bàn 131
because 114
before 113
behind 147–8
bèi 9, 105
bǐ 8, 138–40
biān 146–52
bìdìng 59–60
bié 27, 69, 86

bìxū 75–6
both 63, 109–10
不 bù 25–6, 54, 79–80
  with questions 28–9, 55
部 bù 151
búdàn … érqiě 109–10
búguò 111, 114–5
but 107–11
búyào 69
by 102, 105

cái 61, 66, 116
capitalization 42–3
cardinal numbers 8, 117–19
chàbùduō 122
cháng(cháng) 60
characters 13–21
Chinese writing system 13
choice-type questions 36–7
chúfēi … cái 116
chúfēi … yàobùrán … jiù 116
chúle 104–5
clause 8
cohesive conjunctions 110–13
common nouns 41–2
comparison 8, 138–45
complements 88–94
  directional complements 85,
    92–3
  potential complements
    93–4

complements of degree
  88–9
complements of result
  86, 89–92
completed actions 80–3
completed experiences 80,
  83–4
conditional 8, 115
cóng 96–7
cónglái méi 60–1
conjunctions 8, 106–16
coordinating conjunctions
  106–9
correlative conjunctions
  109–10
cuò 91
currency 129–30

dàgài 59
dànshì 111, 114–5
dào 33, 91, 97–8, 103
dàodǐ 61–2
date 133–5
days of the week 134–5
得 de with questions 34
  with directional complements
    88–9
  with potential complements
    94
的 de with questions 37
  as relative pronoun 49–50

highlighting the noun 43–4
with adjectives 52
with location 150
with possessive
pronouns 48–9
with reflexive pronouns 48
deduō 139
de shíhòu 111–12
děi 75–6
decimal point 121
demonstratives 8
demonstrative adjectives 51
demonstrative pronouns
50–1, 124
地 dì 63
第 dì 119–20
direct object 8, 84–5
direction 98, 148–52
distance 97–9, 130
division 120–1
dǒng 90
dōu 57, 61, 63–4, 78
duì 91, 99–100
duìmiàn 147
duìyú 103
duō 123, 132
duō + adjective 32, 34
duō + adverb 32, 34
duō cháng shíjiān 32, 35
duō jiǔ 32, 35
duōle 139
duōme 56, 70
duōshǎo 32, 35

either 36–7
enough 54, 132
enumerative comma 21, 122
èr 117, 125
ér 107–9
except 104
exclamatives 8, 70–2
expressions of quantity
124–32
expressions of time 82,
133–7

family names 42–3
fānér 111
fēicháng 56–7
few 132
for 95, 98, 101
fǒuzé 111
fractions 121
from 96–9
future 81–2

gāng 58
ge 9, 41, 124–5
gěi 95, 101, 105
gēn 100, 106, 141–2

gèng 56, 139–40
gēnjù 103
gòu 54, 132
guānyú 104
guò 7, 61, 80, 83

H

hái 58, 107–8
háishì 36–7, 112
háiyǒu 106–7
half 131
hǎo 91
he 45
hé 106–7
hěn 56, 70
her 45
hers 48
him 45
his 48
hòu 146–8
hòulái 113
hours 135–6
how 32–7, 56–7
how about 38
how long 32, 35
how much/many 32, 35–6
huì 75–7, 90
human nouns 42
huò 36–7
huòxǔ 59
huòzhě *see* huò

I

I 45
ideograms 17
if 65, 114–6
imperative 8, 27, 67–70, 85
impersonal
    constructions 24
in 33, 96, 146–48
indefinite past 80, 83
indirect object 9
inference conjunctions 112
infinitive 9
intensifiers 89
interrogative 9
interrogative pronouns
    30–2
it 24, 45, 47
its 48

J

jǐ 32, 35–6, 123
jiàn 90
jiào 68–9, 105
jīngcháng 60
jìrán … jiù 114–5
jíshǐ … yě 114–5
jiù 58, 61, 64–5, 112,
    114–16
jiūjìng 61
just 58

kāishǐ 97
kěndìng 59–60
kěnéng 59
kěshì 111, 114–5
kěyǐ 75–8
kuài *see* kuàiyào
kuàiyào 83

la 71
lái 92–3, 97, 123, 143
language 13
lǎoshì 60
le 7, 27, 69, 80–5, 143
less 131, 144
lǐ 146–8
lí 99
liǎng 117, 125
lìngwài 107–8
listing conjunctions 112–3
location words 22–3,
    146–52

ma 28–9, 55
  with rhetorical questions 39
  with tag questions 40
Mandarin 13
many 132

mathematical expressions
    120–1
me 45
measure words 9, 41–2, 120,
    124–32
measurements 129–30
méi negating possession
    26, 74
  negating the past tense 26
  negative comparison 138,
    140–1
  with bǎ 87
méiyǒu *see* méi
men 42
miàn 146–52
mine 48
minutes 135–6
modal verbs 9, 75–9, 86
months 133–4
more 56, 131, 143–5
most 142–3
much 139
multiplication 120–1
my 48

nà 50–1, 124
nǎ 30–3
na 71
nǎr 32–3
nàme 141
names 42–3, 74

nándào 39
nationality 74
nàxiē 50–1
nǎxiē 30, 32
ne with choice-type
  questions 36
 emphatic use 66
 question particle 38
negative commands 27, 69
negative expressions 25–7,
  54, 79
néng 75, 77–8
never 60–1
nǐ 45
nǐde 48
nǐmen 46
nǐmende 49
nín 45–6
nínde 48
no 29
non-human nouns 42
not 109–10
noun phrases 43–4
nouns 9, 22, 41–4
number 9
numbers 117–23

oneself 47
ongoing actions 84
only 57, 65–6, 109–10
or 36–7
ordinal numbers 9, 119–10
our 49
ours 49
out 146–8

object 9, 22
object pronouns 45–7
of 121
on 33, 96, 146–8

páng 146–8
passive voice 9, 105
past participle 10
past tense 37, 80–4
percentages 121
person 10
personal pronouns 10, 45–9
pictograms 17
pinyin 10, 20, 43
plural 10, 41
p.m. 136
polite imperatives 67
possessive 10
possessive pronouns 48–9
prepositions 10, 23, 95–105
prices 129–30
profession 54, 74
pronouns 11
pronunciation 13–14, 18,
  20–1
proper nouns 42–3
punctuation 21, 122

qián 146–8
qǐng 67
qīngchǔ 92
qù 92–3, 97
quán 57
quantity 124–32
questions 28–40, 55

radicals 18–19, 153–60
ràng 68–9, 105
ránhòu 112–3
reflexive 11, 47–8
reflexive pronouns 47–8
relative pronouns 49–50
réngrán 58
rénmen 42
rhetorical questions 39–40
rúguǒ ... jiù 8, 114–5

semantic-phonetic
   compounds 18
sentence 11
shàng 146–8
shàngxià 122
she 45–6
shéi 30
shéide 30

shénme 31
shì 53–4, 64, 74
   with location 152
   with rhetorical questions 39
shì ... de 37
shífēn 56–7
shìfǒu 29
should 75–6
shuí see shéi
similarity 141–2
simplified characters 15
since 96–7, 115
singular 11, 41
so 56–7, 110
some 131
stative verbs 11, 73–4
still 58
strokes 14–16
subject 11, 22
subject pronouns 45–7
subordinating conjunctions
   113–16
subtraction 120–1
such 70
suīrán ... kěshì/dànshì/búguò
   114–5
superlative 11, 142–3
surnames 43

tā 45–7
tag questions 40
tài 56

tāmen 46–7
tāmende 49
tèbié 56–7
telephone numbers 119
tenses 12, 80–4, 136–7
that 49–51
their 49
theirs 49
them 46–7
then 65, 111–13
there is/there are 24
these 50–1
they 46–7
this 50–1
those 50–1
tì 102
time 22–4, 36, 133–7
time-linking conjunctions
    111–2
to 33, 97–99
to be 53–4, 74
tones 12, 20–1
tóng 106–7
too 56, 64, 83, 106–7
topicalization 12, 23
tou 146–8
towards 98–9
traditional characters 15

under 146–8
unless 66, 116

until 66, 98
us 46

verbal measure words 128
verbs 12, 22–3, 53–5, 73–87
voice 12

wa 71–2
wài 146–8
wán 90
wǎng 98
we 46
weather 24
wèi 101–2
weight 130
wèile 103
wèishénme 32–3
what 30–1
when 37, 111–12
where 32–3
whether 29
which 30–2, 49–50
while 110
who 30, 49–50
whom 30, 49–50
whose 30, 49–50
why 32–3
with 100
wǒ 45

wǒde 48
wǒmen 46, 68
wǒmende 49
word order 22–4
words 19

xià 146–8
xiàng 98
xiǎngyào 75, 78
xūyào 75, 78

ya 71
yào 75, 78, 82
yàobùrán 111
yě 107–8
yě ... yě 109
years 133
yědōu 64
yes 29
yes/no questions 28–9
yěxǔ 59, 62
yìbiān ... yìbiān 109–10
yìdiǎn 131, 139
yídìng 59–60
yígòng 57
yǐhòu 113
yǐjīng 58, 82
yīncǐ 110
yīnggāi 75–6

yīnwèi ... suǒyǐ 114
yìqǐ 57
yǐqián 113
yǐshàng 123
yǐxià 123
yìxiē 131
yíyàng 100, 141–2
yìzhí 58
you 45–6
yòu 60
yòu ... yòu 109
yǒu to have 26, 74
  there is/there are 24, 74, 151–2
  as emphasis 34
  with questions 29
yóu 102
your 48–9
yours 48–9
yǔ 106–7
yuànyì 75, 78
yuè ... yuè 143–5

再 zài 60
在 zài 33, 96, 150–2
zánmen 46, 68
zánmende 49
zěnme 32–4
zěnmeyàng 32–4
zero 117
zhè 50–1, 124
zhe 7, 80, 84–5

zhēn 56, 70
zhèng *see* zhèngzài
zhèngzài 58, 84
zhèxiē 50
zhǐ 57
zhǐyào ... jiù 114–5
zhǐyǒu ... cái 116

zhìyú 104
zhōngjiān 147
zhù 91
zìjǐ 11, 47–8
zǒngshì 60
zuì 11, 142–3
zuǒyòu 122